Sept. 8th '01.

Joan Swann.

NOEL

NOEL

23.9.51–10.10.79

Joan Swann

The Book Guild Ltd
Sussex, England

First published in Great Britain in 2001 by
The Book Guild Ltd
25 High Street
Lewes, East Sussex
BN7 2LU

Copyright © Joan Swann 2001

The right of Joan Swann to be identified as the author of
this work has been asserted by her in accordance with the
Copyright, Designs and Patents Act 1988.

All right reserved. No part of this publication may be reproduced,
transmitted, or stored in a retrieval system, in any form or by any means,
without permission in writing from the publisher, nor be
otherwise circulated in any form of binding or cover other than that in
which it is published and without a similar condition being imposed on
the subsequent purchaser.

Typesetting in Times by
IML Typographers, Birkenhead, Merseyside

Printed in Great Britain by
Bookcraft (Bath) Ltd, Avon

A catalogue record for this book is available from
The British Library.

ISBN 1 85776 543 5

CONTENTS

1	The Beginning	1
2	People and Places	7
3	Melanie	15
4	School	19
5	Hospitals and Staff	22
6	Oxford	36
7	Southmead – Revisited	45
8	Food and Drink	52
9	Toys and Entertainment	57
10	Work	66
11	Sport	70
12	Religion	74
13	Holdays and 'Special Days'	79
14	Clothes and Personal Belongings	85
15	... And Lovely Things	89
16	The Final Tally	95

1

The Beginning

'Go home and complete your family, then I'll do something for you.'

Those were the words uttered by a very well-known West Country gynaecologist who had been treating me for a prolapse of the womb since the birth of our first child – a healthy girl. Melanie, at the time those famous words were spoken, was 15 months old, so we decided to follow his advice and I became pregnant virtually overnight!

Little did I know what lay ahead or how those words would affect all our lives. The following nine months I certainly didn't feel as well as I had during my first pregnancy and I had a fluctuating temperature all through – which my doctor told me to stop fussing about. (He is long since dead – but in any case those were his words.) I realised very early on that I felt totally different from when I was carrying Melanie – but I couldn't get through to anybody - and I was fobbed off with 'You're just over-anxious' – and nothing was done.

There was a very real fear deep down within me of having a haemophiliac child – if I had a boy – as this strain ran in our family. My mother had lost a brother with this condition and then had two boys herself with the same deficiency disorder – one of them dying at the age of two. The hereditary pattern is that only the males have it but the females have about a fifty-fifty possibility of being a carrier.

Why on earth with this family history did we try our luck? Well, my eldest sister had married (she was 20 years older than me and had never had children) and my other sister had been blessed with two healthy normal boys – surely we'd be lucky too? It must be missing a generation or so we kept telling ourselves.

The degree of haemophilia can vary tremendously from a slight tendency to bleed abnormally to a very severe deficiency of the vital blood-clotting factors, causing major bleeds. I'd had quite an insight into all the problems involved as my surviving haemophiliac brother was living with us in the family home, plus my father (my mother had died many years previously).

My pregnancy went full-term and our second baby was born at home – it was a boy – and I had an immediate premonition that trouble lay ahead. It did. From the very first the baby wouldn't suckle, even when I knew he was starving and I was exuding milk like a Friesian cow. He looked reasonably normal but on the second day became severely jaundiced – for which he received no treatment, it just had to run its course. It wasn't so much his looks that perturbed me but his behaviour pattern. Having had a normal child first, obviously I was able to make comparisons, and when he didn't gain weight. and remained very lethargic I became more and more concerned. I literally sat for hours trying to get him to feed and his intake was almost negligible – as my milk-bar indicated in no uncertain terms.

I kept repeating like a parrot to my doctor, the health nurse and anyone else who would listen 'I'm sure my baby isn't normal' – but no one would go along with me. Even my husband thought I was over-reacting and said 'I expect boys are slower than girls!' After three months of nearly going insane with worry I insisted on another opinion and eventually got an appointment to see a paediatrician at the Children's Hospital, Bristol

I will never forget that day. Having no transport of our own I travelled down by bus and met my mother-in-law at the bus station. She came to the hospital with me The waiting before going in seemed interminable and bad enough, but the coming out was worse. (By this time Noel was bruising just with normal handling, so while expecting to hear the word 'haemophiliac' I hadn't consciously attached a category to his backwardness.) So imagine my feelings when the haemophilia was confirmed and then I was told he was a mongol (as Down's Syndrome sufferers were then called) – but a reasonably high-grade one. I walked round the streets of Bristol for a good half-hour with my mother-in-law before I could bring myself to tell her what had been diagnosed. The journey home seemed endless and I dreaded the thought of having to tell my husband – though I guessed he would take one look at my face and know something was up.

Bad though the news was, even as early as on my journey home I now had something positive with which to contend. At least there would be no more dreadful weeks of not knowing and heart-searching, and whatever the future held we'd try and cope with it as a family. Acceptance of the situation was the first major hurdle over. Little did we know then that fate had some even crueller blows in store for Noel and us. Further tests at the Children's Hospital proved without doubt that he was a very bad haemophiliac.

When I discussed the situation with my own GP I asked him why he'd kept fobbing me off, and his reply was that he'd been trying to protect me from knowing for as long as possible. How very wrong he was – 'the known, however bad, is never as frightening as the unknown' – and how little he knew me. I need to know, then I dig my heels in – and fight! I didn't wait for people to look in the pram and commiserate with or pity us. I just told everyone Noel was one of life's unfortunates and we were going to try our hardest to give him as good a life as possible.

Our local welfare clinic, which I attended regularly with Noel, proved to be a tremendous help. It was through them he was put on Adexalin because he couldn't take cod-liver oil, and very, very gradually he started to gain weight. That was one step forward – but in between feeds he just lay in his pram not reacting to noise, movement or anything going on around him. Even Melanie, a lively two-year-old, had no affect upon him whatsoever. Of course she was very interested in her new brother but it was so difficult to stop her cuddling him too enthusiastically or bouncing the pram too energetically. She had always been such a live wire herself as a baby and I'd oft said, 'I wish I had a placid baby' – now, in Noel I had one that was too placid. Two babies in the same family couldn't have been more poles apart.

Poor Noel had such a bad start – not even getting the name I'd chosen for him! I wanted him to be called Digby, and insisted this should be so, but when my husband returned from registering him he said, 'He's registered as Noel after my second name!' It was too late for me to do anything about it and somehow over the years 'Noel' seemed right, unless he went by his nickname of 'Titch'.

We struggled – that being the operative word – through the early months of his life, ever searching for any small improvement or accomplishment, but often weeks and months went by with very little to break the daily routine. It was a great day when we propped him up in his pram and he didn't flop over! Very gradually his muscle tone improved – and he didn't feel quite so much like an India-rubber ball. He was almost a year before he could sit up on his own. We were very thrilled when we found he was beginning to look at things around him, and there was a semblance of a smile at times – but there were no sounds as yet that meant anything, though we persevered for hours with Da-da, Mum etc.

When he started to crawl, very unconventionally, life became a nightmare. There were so many bumps causing bad bruising – all we could do was to keep him in dungarees and protect him as much as possible. When he walked, at nearly two, even more problems presented themselves – as he became more mobile so the bleeds got worse.

He cut his teeth very late, and not at all according to the norm, often cutting a back one and then a front one. He bled copiously with each one. It was even worse when he lost his baby teeth before his permanent ones came.

His first sojourn in hospital for a major bleed was when he was just over a year old. It was Christmas-time and he'd started a bleed into his face as we thought, but when he found difficulty in swallowing we guessed it had gone to his throat. This was the first transfusion he had. I'm glad we didn't know then how much time he'd spend on the end of a 'drip'. Being an odd blood-group didn't help either. The second time he was admitted to the Children's Hospital it was for a more serious bleed. He had bled into a body cavity and was in extreme pain in the abdominal area. He was rushed in by ambulance as an emergency and the journey down to Bristol was a nightmare. The Filton Hill terrain was always the worst part of the journey – the potholes and bumps made it like a switchback – and I spent my time trying to hold Noel in as comfortable a position as possible. Once again a fresh-blood transfusion stopped him bleeding.

At that stage of his life, in 1952, the vital clotting factor hadn't been extracted. In latter years he had literally gallons of Cryoprecipitate by transfusion. This was the missing factor he needed – but when he'd had a massive bleed of course he required the full blood straight from a donor. We often thought of the unknown people who saved him time and time again. Blood donors should receive more acclaim.

His hospital stays were particularly worrying to us when he was young as his vocabulary was so limited and he used his own made-up words to ask for what he wanted. Being with him all the time we gradually built up an understanding of his needs and never missed a day visiting and helping as much as we could. Parent participation wasn't really the 'in thing' during his early years, but we usually found the hospital staff were very appreciative of what we did.

Soon Noel's pattern of life was established – home, where he was cocooned as much as possible from bleeds and his frequent trips to hospital. If he had only been a mongol, life would have been comparatively easy for us all but it was the pain caused by the internal bleeds into joints and other parts of the body that took its toll of him and us.

As the years went by Noel's own little personality developed and his courage and endurance made us love him even more. I think him being a mongol was really a blessing in disguise. I'm sure it saved his sanity – with all he had to put up with (the excruciating pain of his numerous bleeds – and worst of all his four amputations for 'bone-cysts'). A person of normal intelligence would probably have ended it all.

I suppose a tragedy like Noel could split a family asunder – but I truly believe it made us all closer. There were times when it was very hard and tough going but through it all our love helped him and us. Perhaps the greatest compliment we ever received was when an old friend of ours said we'd 'turned a tragedy into a blessing'.

This isn't going to be a book on just ill-health and suffering. I think there'll be a fairly good mixture of pathos and humour. As I didn't want to write a saga of Noel's life from birth to death I've approached it through the different people and places that encompassed him, and the pleasures that came to him from the simple things in life.

2

People and Places

So many people affected Noel's life – but it soon became apparent from about the age of two that his daddy and I were his 'sun, moon and stars. However short a time we were away from him we received such a welcome on return; and when he was able to talk it was invariably 'me missed you'. Melanie too was adored by him and in his eyes could do no wrong. In later years if we grumbled at Mel Noel always took her part saying, 'Melanie's a good girl.' As I mentioned previously my father lived with us and he and Noel were real buddies. Melanie and her Grampy never quite hit it off – but Noel and Grampy did. Grampy was always called 'Old Dad'. He introduced Noel to his first taste of alcohol! This consisted of draught cider on a cork – secreted round in the summer-house. I didn't cotton on for a time as to what was going on till in passing one day I heard Noel saying, 'More Old Dad' – and investigated!

Old Dad, although retired, was a very early riser and from about the age of four Noel, as soon as he heard him, crept downstairs to join him. I must say my father had lots of patience with Noel – more than he'd ever had with any of us.

When our children were young the old A38 ran right outside our house – so our tall iron gate had a chain on the top for safety. On the very odd occasion when this was inadvertently left off, Noel would toddle down to the pub to find 'Old Dad'! One really needed eyes everywhere to keep tabs on him.

Uncle Bert (as mentioned, himself a haemophiliac) was a great favourite with Noel. One would say they had a special empathy between them. He helped Noel tremendously with his speech and when he was older taught him to tell the time. This meant such a lot to him as he then knew what time Mummy came home from school, Daddy home from work, and particularly the times of his favourite TV programmes!

Noel was indeed fortunate in always having lots of people around him, talking to and encouraging him to make sounds and new words. We tried to include him in everything we did as far as possible and as his health permitted. I suppose it is true to say he became the focal point of our home. We rejoiced with him when he was well and suffered with him to a degree when he was ill.

So where did Melanie feature in this set-up? As she was an intelligent little girl and very independent, we probably treated her as being older than she was. (Maybe more books should be written about the brothers and sisters of handicapped children.) Amazingly enough she grew up with a very protective feeling towards Noel and never seemed to resent all the extra time and attention given to him. She was always a 'Daddy's girl' though, so didn't lack love. She knew we loved her but perhaps at times we over-compensated her money-wise with clothes, toys and outings etc.

I suppose we couldn't have done too many things wrong as thank God, she grew up a well-balanced child.

Being a member of a large family myself, I provided Noel with plenty of real aunts and uncles and by the time he was five he'd got them all sorted out as to who was who even if he couldn't say all their names properly. Aunty Phyllis was 'Aunty Pill', Aunty Ruth became 'Woof with the black hair'; Uncle David – 'Da-id'; Uncle Ralph – 'Walf'. Uncle George – 'Orge, velly funny', (he was a real comedian and used to have Noel in stitches!) and my eldest sister 'Aunty Eva – velly soft!' (This was because she often wore a coat with a large fur collar and Noel loved stroking it.) Her husband, 'Uncle Bill', visited us every Sunday and stayed for tea. Noel used to get so agitated if Bill were a few minutes late and would never have it that Uncle Bill belonged to Melanie too – 'It's my Uncle Bill.' Noel loved a regular pattern of visitors, particularly during his immobile years.

I would say that the two people, other than family, Noel was particularly fond of were the ones who looked after him when I returned to teaching. I'd had ten years 'out', so when I went back Melanie and Noel were at school also. These two wonderful people helped me out for the rest of Noel's lifetime. This is how they got their names!

There was a person who had previously worked part-time for me, and Noel was quite fond of 'Aunty Betty' – but often got reprimanded for ambling off with her polish and hiding her dusters or tipping up the dustpan! She decided to leave and another 'Aunty' came. To Noel everyone was either an 'Aunty' or an 'Uncle' – so on seeing the new one he exclaimed 'More Aunty'. This remained her name for always.

The name he gave to the person who came to help 'More Aunty' out when she herself became ill was quite spontaneously given, though we never knew why. He just said 'You, Top Cat' – and that stuck!

More Aunty and Top Cat each loved Noel and he reacted to them in such different ways. More Aunty he tended to be very gentle with, always asking her if she was all right even when he was ill himself. Top Cat gave him his lighter moments. He teased her and at times he was quite wicked. There was a fantastic rapport between them. Noel would declare he was boss, and then the fun started. From this came her second nickname of 'Bossy Billy'.

They were both so kind with him when he had a bleed – but of course I stayed home with him or my husband did when he was really ill and needed us or if he had to go to hospital. Top Cat was our 'sitter' when my husband and I had the occasional evening out. We went, knowing we couldn't leave Noel in safer hands.

I'm sure one of Noel's earliest memories must have been of the lovely young girl in the village who had just started her first job after leaving school. She gave up her half-day every week to take Noel out in the pram and fetched him every Sunday morning to take him down to their family farm. Her delight when he learnt a new word or recognised an animal and tried to emulate its noise was almost as great as his. She had beautiful blonde hair which seemed to fascinate Noel. Her name being Doreen, she became 'Aunty Dor-Dor' and her parents later on were always 'Aunty and Uncle Jones'.

The farm dogs were wonderfully gentle with him, almost as if they knew they had to be. He took a great fancy to Carlo and often had snaps taken with him. The name 'Jones' had a special significance during Noel's lifetime. More about that later...

The children in the village tended to fall into two categories – those who were rather wary when viewing Noel in his invalid chair and those who wanted to push him and endeavour to make him laugh. After the first two years of his life it soon became evident he was developing quite a good sense of humour – and when the other children gambolled and cavorted around he chuckled almost uncontrollably. Often we had to stop the antics for fear of him hurting himself. We were never allowed to pass the village shop without him seeing 'Aunty Smart' and being on the receiving end of sweets or ice-cream.

One of his favourite vantage spots when he was still able to get about under his own steam was the garden gate. He invariably (in fine weather) carried his potty there to perform, much to the amusement of passers-by! He received innumerable sticks of rock from holiday makers returning home and having a last fling at the hotel opposite. We had to be very diplomatic removing the rock from him as it was much too splintery for him to eat.

There were also his 'regulars' who visited him at the gate. They ranged from teenagers who brought him presents to the older generation, who could always find time to spare to chat to him. Of course the tradespeople who called were all treated as old friends. We had to be very firm about the gate being shut and the chain put on, entering and leaving, else given the slightest chance Noel was away. Melanie spent quite a lot of her time retrieving him!

The paperman, the breadman and coalman were very firm favourites of his. They had their moments of fun and happiness with him when he was well and showed genuine sorrow when he was in a bad patch and suffering.

One person who can never be forgotten by us was our laundryman who called on us each week for many, many years. Noel always insisted he should have a cup of coffee in his room. (This was during the years he was confined to bed.) There is no doubt it was his highlight of the week, especially as the laundryman always brought him a packet of Smarties – nothing else would do – and there was quite a lot of teasing before they were finally produced from one pocket or another. When he himself was extremely ill and off work for months his relief man still brought Noel his Smarties. Fortunately he got better and was able to take up his job again – and Noel was beside himself with joy when he called on us again, saying, 'Me very happy you better.'

The kindness of people like this makes one feel very humble. I don't know where he is now as the laundry service to this area was withdrawn. He may not even know Noel is no longer with us, but we always remember him as one of Nature's gentlemen – in the truest meaning of the word.

Yet another visitor who came at regular intervals during Noel's 'laid-up' years was our hairdresser friend. When Uncle Johnny arrived Noel viewed him rather apprehensively – watching intently as the instruments of torture came out of the bag!

He never really got over his dislike of having his hair cut, but at least sat as immobile as the Sphinx. There were times when he had to be 'done' lying down. What a performance! Johnny (all six foot of him) had to kneel to make contact. Noel was swathed in towels and plastic sheets – yet hair still turned up in the most odd crevices! The look of relief on his face when the 'operation' was complete, and the big sigh, followed by 'All done now', usually raised a laugh.

Then came the washing! Daddy held the bowl at the back of his head while I administered the shampoo and did the rinsing. Not enjoyed by Noel. Fortunately there was a happy ending; he loved having it dried with his own hand electric hair dryer – which he called his 'burr-burr'. (Aunty Woof with the black hair still makes use of it.)

These evenings required rather a mammoth effort from the team – but it was reward enough when all was serene again to hear Noel ask, 'You do think me lubbly now?'

Noel of course from a very early age came into contact with nurses and doctors. They figured largely in his life, but obviously our local GPs were the ones he came under most. We were exceptionally lucky in them, most of the time. We people who are so to say 'normal' think we reason and work things out logically, but so often Noel did the correct thing from sheer instinct. From a very early age he recognised authority and knew that 'Uncle Doctor' was trying to help him. Once Noel gave his love to anyone, it was given for life.

He was extremely loyal and no one could budge him – however much we teased him. One of our GPs was a Scot and we knew from the word go he was 'the one' with Noel. (He came into his life when Noel was about 12.) We all pretended we thought the others were the best – and not the one in question – but Noel would shake his head and say, 'Me love Dr W,' and until the day he unfortunately left for another practice Noel never changed in his feelings. I'm glad he was with us through some of the worst years in Noel's life. Even as the years went on and he grew to be fond of other doctors he never forgot Dr W and always said he loved him best. One who came for just a short time, fortunately, Noel dubbed as 'Not too bad'. He wasn't far wrong in his judgement either!

I mustn't leave out another person who featured largely in Noel's life. He visited him regularly through the latter years when he was confined to bed. This was our vicar. He was very tickled when Noel christened him 'the man with the collar' – and it stuck! When he sent Noel cards during his hospital stays, this is how he signed himself. Even when Noel spent a long period in the Nuffield Orthopaedic Hospital at Oxford, the Canon, as I should correctly call him, visited him there, and when Noel was getting better the ward echoed to the sound of 'The man with the collar's come to see me'.

We always believe that thanks to 'the man with the collar' a minor miracle occurred. An exceptionally bad bleed into the bicep of his left arm kept Noel in Southmead Hospital, Bristol, for nearly two months. The intensity of this bleed paralysed his arm and we were given very little hope of it ever recovering. When he returned home he wasn't in pain but his arm was completely immobile. Although we did all we could in the way of encouragement and giving him a soft ball to rest his hand on in the hope his fingers would start to move – it was all to no avail. It made moving him around so much more difficult too. After nine months there was no improvement.

Now, how did 'the man with the collar' come in on this? Well he had enlisted the services of Alan Taylor at the opening of the church fête and on hearing this I said to the Canon, 'Noel would be beside himself if he saw Alan Taylor – he adores his programme.'

His *Tinkertainment* programme was delightful and the grown-ups fell for his *Mr & Mrs* programmes on ITV as well. Without more ado he set things in motion and it was arranged. We kept it a complete surprise from Noel and his pleasure had to be seen to be believed when Alan Taylor walked in! He stayed and talked to him for about 20 minutes or so. When he left, Noel kept saying, 'Me saw Alan Taylor, very lubbly man!' Less than half an hour after he left our house, Noel raised his hand about an inch off the bed! I stared in amazement, hardly able to believe my eyes. That was the beginning of recovery, and in about two more months the arm was reasonably mobile. It never completely recovered, having only limited movement in the elbow joint – but there was such an improvement. But for the Canon Noel would never have met Alan Taylor. Call it coincidence if you like that it happened when it did – we tend to believe otherwise.

Throughout Noel's lifetime, particularly the latter years, we derived a lot of pleasure from people visiting us, as it was difficult to plan anything in advance with Noel's bleeds being so spasmodic and spontaneous – and we weren't able to be very 'outgoing' ourselves.

Again, people fell into two categories: those who wanted to know – and those who didn't. Some perhaps were too embarrassed to come and see us, or maybe felt that as they had normal children we would feel resentful. Those that made the effort soon knew it was worthwhile. I can truthfully say we never felt bitter about our lot and when Noel was free from pain he was an absolute tonic.

I've seen friends of ours laugh till the tears ran down their cheeks at some of his antics. He was quite a good little mimic. Here's a 'for instance'. Melanie brought him back a fez from a Tunisian holiday. The minute he clapped eyes on it he announced, 'Oh good! Me Tommy Cooper' and did the appropriate arm actions! As this was after his amputation which left him with just a little stump below the elbow on the one arm, it was rather like an elephant's trunk waving around! He really used to put on quite a little show.

One of our friends who visited us every Thursday evening for many years never escaped without putting on a 'keep-fit display' for Noel. This originated from the time he told her she had 'a big fat belly and bum'. To which she replied, 'I shall have to do some exercises then.' These included floor ones, with legs in the air cycling, the crab position, bending to touch toes and head and arm exercises, etc. etc. This display Daddy enjoyed quite as much as Noel!

Perhaps one of the highest attributes Noel ever gave anyone was that he or she had a 'fatty face'. This meant that in his eyes they were 'very super'. Another of our friends, a very close one, had the same name as his Aunty Ruth – and she was nicknamed immediately 'Aunty Woof with the fatty arms'! They enjoyed many cuddles together. Noel always seemed to latch on to some positive thing about the person when dubbing them with their nickname.

One of the headmasters I worked under was a true friend in need. Many was the time he took me to hospital to see Noel, when we hadn't any transport of our own. He was a big man with a hearty laugh and another firm favourite of Noel's. His name was Pratt – and until Noel was able to sound his R's he and his wife were 'Uncle and Aunty Fat'!

He had two friends both called Maureen, so they became 'Little Aunty Maureen' and 'Big Aunty Maureen from over the wall'.

We can never be grateful enough to all the people who over the years helped us to have some lighter moments.

3

Melanie

I think Melanie warrants a chapter to herself, as apart from how she felt towards Noel, he had a profound effect upon her life. I was always glad she'd had the first two years being our 'sole target' for love. Any child when a new babe arrives feels their nose has been put out of joint a bit – but it was much worse for Mel as Noel took up so much of our time. The first year of his life when he was just a baby – and not expected to do much – wasn't too bad, but when her friends who had baby brothers and sisters were able to play with them and she couldn't with Noel, it became rather confusing for her. Also the fact, as time went on, that she got a smack if she were naughty but Noel didn't. Our patience was often stretched to the limit coping with him, and there really wasn't much left for Mel, who, being a normal inquisitive and rather mischievous child, often needed correcting.

She missed so much the rough and tumbles she would have had with a normal brother, but by about four had accepted the situation and become very protective towards him – and Noel was developing feelings towards Melanie. It upset her a lot when he was in bad pain and cried, and I'm sure there were lots of times when we weren't very approachable when we'd had a series of bad nights up with him. All minor bleeds we coped with at home, with the aid of painkillers taken orally (prescribed by our GP). Noel was simply terrified of the needle and being on the end of a drip, and he remained this way till the end of his life. This is why we probably tried to keep him out of hospital as much as we could – but always knowing that if a bleed became progressively worse he would have to be admitted. Melanie didn't like the ambulance arriving and invariably wept with him.

Our daily visits to hospital were usually in the early evening, unless there was an emergency, so nine times out of ten, during the early years, someone else had to put Melanie to bed and read her bed-time story. There were the periods when Noel had a reasonably good patch without bad bleeds and life seemed wonderful then – believe me, we made the most of it, though we did tend to feel we lived on top of a volcano, always wondering when it was going to erupt. Our friends said there was never any need to ask how Noel was as we reacted like a barometer to his state of health.

When the time came for Noel to go to an occupational centre, at the age of six, Melanie just couldn't understand why he wasn't able to go to her school – yet she accepted that he was backward. The first sentence Mel ever said was, 'Melanie can do it' and this attitude came up again when we explained to her in more detail why Noel had to go to a special school. She kept saying over and over again, 'But I'll look after him – I know I can.' I remember how proud she was the first time she was allowed to take him to Sunday school on her own. From about nine she could be trusted to take him out in his chair, though I think he played her up sometimes. It was many years later we heard the complete story of when he fell out into some stinging nettles. She and her friend applied dock-leaves to the affected areas!

Children, like grown-ups vary considerably and there were those in the village who loved going with Mel and Noel round the lanes, but there were a few (in the minority, thank goodness) who taunted Mel with 'Your brother's a nutter.' I still marvel how wonderfully well she turned out, considering everything. She says she never felt unloved as a child – so we must have got something right.

Round the age of six Noel went through a difficult stage when he didn't want to clean his teeth and having his hair washed was a major operation. Mel was usually the one who succeeded in getting round him. He always had to be led, not driven. It was the same with learning new things – Mel was very quick at 'cottoning on' and took great delight when she had success in teaching him something new. She taught him to count with a pack of playing cards. This stood him in good stead when it came to sharing out Easter eggs and sweets etc.

Melanie was usually the one who had to hang on to Noel when family snaps and photos were taken. He simply hated keeping still and looking in the right direction. When he first saw himself in a mirror he was completely bewildered and when confronted with himself in a photo he wouldn't accept it was him. He said, 'It was just a boy.'

We had always impressed on Melanie that she mustn't be ashamed of Noel because he wasn't as lucky as she was to be fit and normal, but she did go through a bad patch during early puberty. She was convinced no boy would want to know her when he found out about Noel. Very fortunately all the boys that came home with her, from the lurex-coated ones to the more stereotypical were all, without exception, fantastic with him.

Mel was 12 when Noel's first foot amputation took place. There were three dreadful months leading up to this, considerable pain for him and mental torture for us. Mel, who had just started grammar school, was shattered. So many times over the years when Mel needed us most we weren't available because we were visiting Noel in hospital. Thank God there were some lighter moments that helped along the way!

Having his hair cut was literally 'hair-raising'. Melanie was responsible for one shaggy cut done with a pair of nail scissors, round in the summer-house! Luckily, the damage was only visual, he wasn't injured in any way – not like the time a genuine hairdresser nicked the top of his ear and there was blood everywhere! Naturally we had to send for the doctor and with pressure pads applied it eventually abated.

As Melanie and Noel grew older they became even closer and Noel was very upset when Mel started her training as a student nurse at the Bristol Eye Hospital. He loved it when she came home, usually bearing some gift for him! Of course we had the usual 'growing-up' scenes with Mel when we seemed to be on to her most of the time and didn't agree with all she did – but where Noel was concerned, she was fantastic.

Whenever he was in hospital, Mel would be there giving us support and helping Noel through some desperate times – and these were numerous. I couldn't count how often we'd been told there was no hope – but Noel was a fighter and by God for many years a survivor. I think we did manage to give him something – I can't put a name to it – which helped him through his many ordeals. We were always there right behind him – even when it came to disagreeing with the medical profession, and quite often we were proved right!

After Melanie married at 19 (much too young, we thought), she and her husband would come and look after Noel for a weekend or so to give us a break. We could go knowing he'd receive every care and attention – but he didn't like us going. On return it was always the same, the shy duck of the head and 'Very happy you home, Mummy'. When Mel's marriage fell apart, Noel couldn't understand what had happened to 'Wobert' – but very much rejoiced in the fact that Mel was once again living at home!

I think I can truthfully say, through all the tough times we remained a family.

4

School

The next group of people who had a tremendous effect upon Noel were those associated with the occupational centre he went to on and off from the age of six. This was situated about 12 miles from our home and necessitated a journey by ambulance each day. Fortunately the head of the centre lived in our village and Noel knew her quite well before he actually started. They hit it off from the word go and he would accept her authority when he wouldn't obey other teachers. He had his stubborn moments like all children – but as I said previously could only be led, not driven.

Mrs Chapman became 'Aunty Wappy' and he adored her. The ambulance drivers were men (and Noel had his favourites among these) and there was a lady in charge to keep control during the journey. I remember there was one of these 'Aunties' who he said was 'A very terrible 'ooman'! I'm quite sure she had never hurt him in any way – but till the time he left he would never say a good word about her. The teachers were always called little or big darlings depending on their size!

Obviously there were long periods of absences when he had bad bleeds but he was always anxious to go back to school and he got a grand reception from the other occupants of the ambulance when he finally made it again. Noel had a favourite girl friend called Bertha, who was a mongol too. Those two were almost inseparable. His other favourite on the ambulance was Ted, who was quite a lot older than he was. Ted had the face of an angel but unfortunately had brain damage. He always wore a cap – which seemed to fascinate Noel as he invariably pulled it off given the slightest chance.

Naturally he had his special favourites among the teachers –

and when he went back to school after his first amputation at the age of 11 wearing his artificial foot, they were truly wonderful – helping him and encouraging him to lead as normal a life as possible. The other children, whatever their own disability, seemed to realise Noel needed more special care than they did. When three years later he had his second amputation and he had a much larger artificial contraption to contend with, the difficulties really arose. It was rather cumbersome and walking on it was such an effort. Although it was specially padded to prevent bleeds, they did occur. Then it was decided that Noel should be lifted into the ambulance in his chair – so a special ambulance fitted with a lift conveyed him to school each day and he remained in his chair except for when he wanted to go to the toilet etc.

One of his special darlings – Miss S – always said how apologetic he was when he asked to be taken to the toilet, and what a nightmare it was to synchronise all the undoings of the straps and paraphernalia with the precise moment as to when he should sit down!

I would have to say that 99 per cent of the ambulance men who collected him were extremely kind and patient and Noel soon had a nickname for most of them too. There was 'Uncle 'ood with the fatty face', 'Black hair with the 'stache', 'Big tall man like my Daddy' and one that really did fit perfectly 'Uncle with the fat belly' (he was rather rotund!).

I know Noel had many happy hours at school and he was learning to read and making progress generally, but there were so many interruptions, due to the haemophilia – it was one setback after another – that eventually his attendance became almost negligible, though we still persevered in sending him when he was able to go.

One of Noel's happiest memories of school was of when he was fit enough to play table-tennis (sitting in his wheelchair) with his darling Miss S. The most poignant memory I have of his school days was a Christmas Nativity play they did and Noel was a shepherd. I don't mind admitting that there was a lump in my throat as they 'sang' their carols.

We still have a little mat that Noel had very laboriously made – he treasured it, as we now do. We often have a smile when we remember the first little poem he ever learnt, with actions. It was called 'The Little Teapot', it was the last line 'Tip me over, pour me out' that really tickled him, and he loved performing it!

He was still at school when he had his third amputation – which didn't prove to be too serious a handicap to him – but when the fourth and last and worst of all came along (more about these amputations later) school became out of the question. So now, even more so, all of Noel's life revolved round home and the people who came to see him there. He never forgot his teachers and friends from school and often talked about his 'darlings'. It was one of his highlights of the year when every Christmas one of his favourite teachers visited him and brought him a present.

After he left school we were still able to take him out occasionally in his specially adapted chair for a few more years when all was well, and if we should chance to meet his ambulance and mates the waves and cheers were ecstatic.

The old saying 'School days are the happiest days of your life' is indeed true in respect of Noel.

5

Hospitals and Staff

Now for the 'nitty-gritty'! So far I haven't gone into any detail of his many visits to hospital – these really were too numerous to count. They began even before he could walk and the first time we left him in the Children's Hospital, Bristol, it was quite heart-breaking. We walked away, as we were requested to do, while his drip was being put up, feeling as though we were deserting him. (In later years we were allowed to stay.) The nursing staff were truly wonderful and I couldn't speak highly enough of them.

He was actually under the care of a woman paediatrician (the same one who had told me what was wrong with him). I don't doubt she was brilliant in her own field – but we always felt she lacked the milk of human kindness. We had many a brush with her during the early years of Noel's life. One of her registrars was a Spaniard who was extremely heavy-handed when examining Noel once when he was in severe pain and I had literally to restrain my husband from knocking him to the ground. Over the years we usually found that the higher up the scale in the medical profession one went, the more understanding and cautious they were in dealing with a haemophiliac – especially one like Noel.

Up to the age of ten Noel's bleeds were typical of his condition – the internal ones being the most painful and dangerous. As I mentioned previously, having lived with my haemophiliac brother I had acquired quite a knowledge of the pattern bleeds took, so when Noel at the age of ten developed an abnormal lump on the top of his left foot which didn't improve with bed-rest and in fact was getting larger and more painful, I became very suspicious that something strange was going on. It was.

(Previous to this at a routine school medical he had been

referred to a specialist at Gloucester, as he was supposedly 'turning his foot over'. No X-rays were taken but it was recommended he wore a caliper. This was duly fitted – on his left leg!)

Several more weeks went by with Noel lying up – all to no avail – and the lump becoming larger, harder and with increased pain. I lived on our doctor's doorstep, on every visit reiterating, 'There's no improvement – what are you going to do about it?' Eventually he decided to X-ray the foot – at Berkeley Hospital. This being only a cottage hospital, the equipment wasn't all it should be – and on viewing the X-ray plate our GP wasn't sure whether there was something wrong with the machine, or what he thought he was seeing was correct. (Our GP told us later one of the bones in the metatarsus group was almost non-existent.) He did move quickly then and we were sent post-haste down to Southmead Hospital, Bristol – to the Outpatient Department.

Here, a very young trainee doctor casually examined Noel and then sent him to have another X-ray of the foot taken. He didn't seem at all perturbed to inform us that Noel had a 'bone-cyst' which could quite easily be dealt with – although he was a haemophiliac. How wrong can one be?

Fortunately, a very well-known orthopaedic specialist was holding an outpatient clinic on the same day. By this time my husband and I were feeling terribly worried and distraught, particularly as Noel was crying with the pain, increased by the extra moving and lifting around. Fate stepped in when Mr David Jones walked in. (He has given me permission to include him in the saga of Noel.) We immediately felt a rapport with him and knew that here was someone who would make some positive decisions. He was so gentle with Noel and had a calming effect on him. After an examination and looking at the X-rays he asked us countless questions – then told us he too considered Noel had a bone-cyst – but was much more dubious about how to deal with it, due to him being a haemophiliac. I know he realised our genuine concern for Noel and did all he could to reassure us that he would 'come up with something'. The first step was to admit him to Southmead Hospital into the children's ward. We took him round there in our car and helped to settle him in. That day we met another wonderful person who was to mean so much to Noel. That was the sister who became 'Tall Sister'. What she gave to those children was way and above the call of duty. She was one in a million. We could never show our gratitude enough. Eventually the time came when we had to leave that evening and as we wended our way homeward, I know we were both wondering whatever would be the outcome.

The days and weeks (four in all) went slowly by, the days seeming so long until we were visiting him, but we were allowed to visit anytime. We never missed a day. Southmead liaised with Oxford, who were the leading authority on haemophilia in the country – and they suggested large quantities of Cryoprecipitate intravenously. This was done, then Noel was virtually up-ended, with his foot suspended in the air. All to no avail; there was no improvement – in fact the swelling had become so massive the decision was made to aspirate to relieve the pressure. All this time the pain was becoming more and more unbearable to Noel, who was on pethidine to alleviate it. The aspirating didn't bring relief. There was no doubt at all Noel's condition was deteriorating – and we dreaded what we would find each time we went down. The nursing staff were wonderfully kind to Noel but they and we knew 'D' day would have to come.

We were sent for yet again to see Mr Jones, who was still dubious about what course to take, and in a moment of complete and utter desperation I said to him, 'But you'll have to do something – even if it means an amputation.' I shall never forget the look on Mr Jones' face. (He told my husband later he'd never forgotten the look on mine at that moment.) After a very prolonged pause came the reply, 'We might just have to – but it will be a difficult decision to make owing to the haemophilia.'

Within a few days we were asked to attend a conference at a nearby orthopaedic hospital at Winford. It would be impossible to say how many specialists were there – but the room was packed. We stayed in with Noel while they all examined his foot and of course a lot of the medical jargon went over the top of our heads. Eventually we took Noel to another room while they discussed at length the problems which lay ahead. After what seemed an interminable time Mr Jones came to tell us that Noel would have to be operated on and he himself would perform the operation, but several more days would have to elapse to prepare him 'blood-wise'. So back we went to Southmead. Once again Noel was on the end of a continual drip. Now the decision had been made, traumatic as it was – we knew what lay ahead of us, but thanked God Noel didn't. He would have the suffering but hopefully the outcome would be successful. The cyst had become so large it was partially stopping the blood flow to the toes and there was fear of gangrene setting in.

The operation was performed on a Sunday, so that the theatre was available for the whole day. It was a hard day to live through – but when we heard he'd made it, we couldn't get down to Bristol quickly enough. We were allowed a peep at him in the intensive care unit; he looked so peaceful though dreadfully pale and of course with the inevitable blood transfusion doing its work. Mr Jones told us the foot had been amputated but he'd been able to leave the heel – which would be an asset to him.

I do not intend to relate in detail all the events that took place in the following weeks of his sojourn at Southmead, but after quite a good start things went awry. Unfortunately his transfusions were stopped too soon and we could see him getting paler, added to which he started sweating profusely (we knew from past experience this was a symptom of bleeding) so once again up went the drip. Unfortunately an unknown and unknowing person when donating their blood hadn't given the information that at some time or other he or she had had jaundice. Noel contracted it. He was whisked into a cubicle on his own and when we visited we had to 'mask and gown-up'. So another setback had cropped up – but eventually, Noel being the trooper and survivor he was, fate opted to be on his side and the day drew nearer for his homecoming.

Noel really adored the senior sister, his 'darling Tall Sister' as he called her, but when she asked him if he wanted to stay with her he said, 'You very lubbly Kister, but me want to go home!' However much the other nurses teased him with, 'You love me best, Noel', he'd shake his head and say, 'me love Kister best!' One nurse actually wrote on his chest in lipstick, 'Noel loves Kister'.

I'm afraid he was rather spoilt during his protracted stay but with all he had to put up with, I think he deserved to be. Mr Jones wore a smile like a Cheshire cat – he was so delighted that Noel had made it and as Noel was the first haemophiliac to have an amputation at Bristol it did much to enhance his reputation. Mr Jones was a brilliant surgeon but by God he was a human being first, caring deeply for others' suffering. Throughout the years he was always 'my darling Mr Jones' to Noel (Amazingly enough he was never called 'Uncle' like the other doctors.)

What a send-off we had as Noel waved goodbye to the children's ward. The tears I hadn't been able to shed over the past months were welling up inside during the journey home. I travelled in the ambulance with Noel and my husband followed in the car. When he was carried into our house he kept looking all around him with sheer rapture on his face. At least we'd got him home, whatever lay ahead – and we knew it could be tough going. However fleeting our happiness was it was a wonderful family reunion.

The first few weeks he was home, he was content to be carried around or just sit – but as time went on he began to get restless and wanted to try to walk. So the problems started. We couldn't clamp down on him completely as it would be a great help to us if he could only move around a little on his own, but we were terrified he'd cause further bleeds into the stump. We had to be very diplomatic and persuasive.

Very gradually his stump hardened and he gained enough confidence to hop around reasonably well with his peg-leg! What a blessing he had his heel. He wore a special stocking made of close-knit firm wool, tubular shaped and with padding in the end for protection. Obviously Mr Jones kept a close check on Noel and we paid regular visits to his clinic. Our main method of getting him from A to B of any distance was either by wheelchair or carrying him out to the car, which was rather heavy going for my husband or myself. Then Mr Jones decided that a specially padded foot and support could be made for him. After the thought came the action, and for many weeks we took Noel to the Artificial Unit Department at Fishponds, Bristol. As I didn't drive in those days, my husband did all the ferrying to and fro. The amount of time he had off work, I wonder he didn't lose his job ten times over. He was wonderful. Yet again we found all the people involved in the Department for artificial limbs really fantastic.

I was there with my husband the first time Noel really walked, without support, 'on his own'! His delight knew no bounds; and he kept saying to everyone, 'Look at my new foot.' That day we took 'the foot', with its support up to the knee, home with us, and very gradually increased the period of time he was able to wear it. We still went to Fishponds for periodic checks – and they were delighted with his progress. He even got to the stage when he could kick a ball and walk up and down steps very satisfactorily. Mr Jones was delighted.

Things really were working out – and we who were involved breathed a sigh of relief. Noel even started back to school – which was a real red-letter day for him. How fleeting happiness is. The next year we got through with the usual crop of bleeds but nothing desperate, and we were grateful for that, added to which he was coping so well with his new foot, though he found it rather hot during the warmer months. Then, right out of the blue, we were in it again – up to our necks!

A bleed, as we thought, had started in the very end of his stump. As this was just a week before we were due to go on holiday to Pra Sands in Cornwall we literally prayed we'd make it. (We'd booked a cottage and would cater for ourselves – so that if Noel were poorly we'd manage between us.) Our own GP came out to see him and wasn't over-perturbed about it being a bad bleed. Noel wasn't in bad pain, so we just kept him lying up with the modicum of tablets – hoping we'd be able to have our holiday. Our stay in Cornwall was to be for two weeks – the first and only time we'd booked for more than a week! When the day for departure came we decided to risk it. So, armed with painkillers of varying strengths up to pethidine we set off.

The journey down was uneventful – Noel was in the back seat, with his leg on a cushion (with Melanie) and didn't complain once of being in pain. Our hopes rose. We knew that when we reached the cottage, which had a garden overlooking the sea, we could carry Noel outside to make him comfortable. Obviously we couldn't put his 'foot' on, that would have been asking for trouble, so he just wore a very loose sock. The first three days he was very quiet for him but didn't complain unduly and we contained the pain with tablets. As the week wore on I knew we weren't going to get away with it. Once again we'd been knocked down to square one. The days and nights were fraught with anxiety and then I dared to utter what was in my mind: surely to God it can't be another bone-cyst?' My husband was more optimistic and kept trying to convince himself and me that all would be well.

Where was poor Melanie while all this was going on? Fortunately for her, the weather was very hot, so she spent her time on the beach, right near the cottage – a lonely figure at times. The heat didn't suit Noel as he sweated so much from the pain. When we had to give him pethidine tablets to keep him reasonably comfortable I knew it was no good, we'd have to return home and in all probability get him into Southmead. We dosed him up well before the journey, but all I can say is, it was a nightmare. We immediately contacted our own doctor on return, and then followed another journey by ambulance to Bristol.

We were grateful there were no delays this time, X-rays were taken the next day, and we were told immediately that yet another bone-cyst had formed and it would mean a further amputation to above the ankle joint. Mr Jones, again, would perform the operation. He told us it was extremely rare for anyone to have more than one bone-cyst, but then Noel never followed 'the norm'.

The saying goes, 'We're never given more than we can bear' but I find this hard to believe. We always had to contend with the mental strain over Noel, but he had the physical suffering to endure, which was often beyond human endurance. So it began, all over again. This time it was a recurring nightmare. He was so desperately ill, we thought it impossible for him to pull through. The one major blessing was that he was in the same ward with his 'darling Kister' and other nurses who remembered him. Yet once more for many, many weeks he was on the end of the inevitable drip. We had to keep our feelings and worry from showing in our faces as Noel hated me to cry. He always said, 'Don't cry, Mummy, be happy.' What a mammoth task that was.

How Noel and we lived through the ensuing couple of months is best forgotten. The continuous transfusions, setbacks, and the haunted look in Noel's eyes. The journeys down to Bristol each evening and virtually staying there nearly all the weekends to be with him every minute we could – it was so sapping. Then there were the nights we stayed as well, when we'd been told yet again there was no hope, and despite everything, including a pulse that was so high it couldn't be charted, he survived! It was incredible, and eventually he once more made the trip home. But what of the future?

We knew it was going to be even more difficult to cope this time – and wondered would there be the remotest chance of fixing him up again with another artificial limb? Noel was getting older and heavier and it was becoming more and more of a problem lifting him around. I was so grateful to have a strong husband. (In later years we often had to enlist the help of our neighbours when I wasn't able to assist.) Several months elapsed before this problem was 'given an airing'. Then began the treks to Fishponds once more – with lots of head scratching and heart searching as to what was best for Noel. The genuine concern and care shown for him made us feel very touched. It was the ultimate.

Eventually they came up with a 'contraption'. It was exceptionally well padded, with strappings up round his waist, but larger and more cumbersome from necessity. This was so that he didn't take too much of his weight on his knee-joint, which would have broken down with bleeds. Oh dear, the problems that arose. He could only wear it for such a short time before we had to take it off. My husband and I were sceptical about it – and Noel hated it – though we tried our hardest to brainwash him into wearing it. It was such a struggle to even get him into it. Balance was one of the major problems, so he was issued with two walking sticks, but these played havoc with his elbow joints and yet more bleeds ensued. (With a haemophiliac there is no part of the body immune from bleeds.)

Fortunately at this time, Noel was issued with an even more modified wheelchair, again fitted with extra padding and a projection that his 'little leg' (as it had become called) rested on. This was mainly for use when not wearing his 'leg' – though there was a period when he was able to attend school that leg and chair were used in conjunction.

At home, we tended more and more to use the wheelchair as the main means of keeping him mobile when well. Unfortunately the 'gear' for his leg started a series of bad bleeds into his thigh – which always meant him being hospitalised. These bleeds were extremely painful – with massive swellings. We wondered more and more if it were worth persevering with the artificial leg. It was after one of these bad do's we decided there was too much risk for Noel, expressed our views, and thankfully the medical bods went along with us – so the leg became obsolete!

Although we'd got rid of one hazard our see-saw pattern of life continued with periods of hope and despondency. Noel loved to be down on the floor, when permissible, and we'd again reverted to the special socks with cotton wool in the end as a safeguard. He'd found he was able to move around on his bottom with his 'little leg' held up using his arms and one leg – but this made him very vulnerable to knocks and bruises, and we could only allow this for very short periods of time. Amazingly enough, Noel had one patch of about six months when he only had minor bleeds and didn't have to be admitted to hospital. We couldn't believe our luck, but we knew even when in a good phase never to get blasé because it couldn't last. It didn't!

Just over a year from his last amputation we were hit for six again. Melanie was cuddling Noel one evening and looking at his nails and teasing him about biting them when she suddenly said, 'Mum, he's got a hard lump in his finger.' It was the finger next to the little one of his right hand. Need I say any more? Truth is indeed stranger than fiction. Same routine, same agonising, X-rays and admittance to the children's ward, Southmead. Mr Jones, as we were, was dumbfounded. Contact was made with all the Western world, in the way of medical records, to see if there was any other case recorded of a person having had three bone-cysts. There wasn't. Noel had made medical history – but who'd want to achieve fame this way?

I don't honestly know why, but my husband and I took this one very badly and Noel was much more upset about losing his finger than he'd been over the foot amputations. I remember so vividly the first words he said when all the dressings eventually came off his hand. He cried dreadfully and said, 'Look what they've done to me, Mummy.' It was so difficult to find words to console him –

and my tears had to be bottled up inside. The only touch of luck was that the finger removed was on his right hand, and he was naturally left-handed, like his father.

As the weeks wore on and he once more gradually improved, his indomitable spirit came through, and towards the end of his stay, when Mr Jones and his retinue came to see him, Noel had them standing in order round his bed; Mr Jones first, then all the 'Uncle' doctors, Kister and nurses and they played catch with his foam ball!

There were lighter moments during Noel's stay for his finger amputation. One lunch-time he was eating his meal – actually he was being fed – when a message came to the ward that Mr Jones wanted to see him immediately in one of the inspection rooms. A staff nurse came along to take him, and as we were there at the time we were told we could go as well.

Noel played up rotten about going, saying he wanted to finish his dinner. At this stage he had a mouthful of meat which was inclined to be rather tough and needed a lot of chewing! We all tried every means we knew to get him to either swallow it or spit it out! All to no avail. He kept repeating it was 'very super!' So, off we went to see Mr Jones and several other consultants with Noel still chewing! Even Mr Jones couldn't get him to abandon it. One hour later when he returned to the ward it was still in his mouth! Until another dinner was produced for him he flatly refused to spit it out.

Amazingly enough, with all we'd been through, it was after Noel's finger amputation that I first saw the chink in my husband's armour. We were driving home along the A38, the first night after he'd had it done, feeling very downcast, when my husband suddenly slammed the brakes on, drew into the side of the road and put his head on the wheel and cried. I guess the dam had to burst sometime and within seconds I too was crying with him unashamedly.

It's funny really what silly things can trigger memories off and cause distress. Several years after Noel's foot amputations I was standing in our school hall while the classes filed in for assembly – I was deep in thought, looking at the ground, and these feet kept going, on and on and on. I cracked wide open and had to get out quickly. I went into the staff-room and it was a good half hour before I could compose myself enough to face my class.

It was after his finger amputation that Noel virtually overnight went off milk and decided all he wanted to drink was Ribena. (I think we should have had shares in this concern, the amount he drank!) He always called it 'Borbena' and this was the name adopted by all the other children in the ward. Every time Noel was admitted to hospital, he took with him a very special pillow, to which he'd formed an attachment. It was a Dunlopillo and he called it his 'Aunty' and invariably cuddled it at night. He was allowed to have this on his bed with his own pillow-case on. While at Southmead Hospital this fact was well known, but when he was transferred later on to an Oxford hospital, 'Aunty' got lost and he was inconsolable. She never turned up again.

I can't speak highly enough of how the doctors, nurses, wardmaids and cleaners treated Noel. He had his favourites in all sections. Obviously there had to be the odd ones he didn't relate to, but usually before he came home each time they were good friends. At first he wasn't sure of the coloured nurses – but once he got used to them he called them 'my darling black face' and they didn't mind one jot!

Once more, after his finger amputation he had a reasonably good patch with only minor bleeds, and we were lulled into a false sense of security. Several months elapsed without him seeing his good friends the ambulance men. They were a wonderful bunch of men – who were real friends in need. Noel always said to them 'Be very careful, don't hurt me,' and their infinite patience and kindness meant so much to us all. The journeys home by ambulance were such a happy affair, with Noel longing to catch the first glimpse of our house, and then shouting 'me home!'

A couple of years passed with very little change in the pattern – happiness and suffering going hand in hand, and his father and I having to do more and more for him. When Noel had had a day free from pain he always said, 'Happy day, Mummy.' We grabbed every moment of happiness we could and appreciated such small pleasures most people would have ignored. A full night's sleep was something to talk about for days – and it was great when he was able to feed himself. (Bleeds into the elbow joints had restricted the arm movement.) We so seldom were able to eat as a family, there was usually one of us helping Noel. Every sunny day when he could be outside was a real bonus day for us, and enjoyed to the full.

I suppose Noel must have been admitted to hospital during almost every hour of the day – but most frequently at night-time. The journeys down to Southmead Hospital with the siren blaring on the ambulance are too numerous to count. I remember so well one very bad night, with icy conditions on the road, at 3 o'clock in the morning, I was in the ambulance with Noel, and my husband was following in our car – the usual procedure. We were really travelling at speed and on looking round to ensure my husband was still with us, I found he wasn't. He had been stopped by a police car! He was asked numerous questions – where he'd come from, home address, had he been drinking, what speed was he doing etc. etc. – but when he said he was on his way to Southmead Hospital and had been following the ambulance with his son in, they were very helpful and even apologetic and escorted him the rest of the way. I don't know if this was because they believed him or not!

So we continued what was for us our normal existence, but always living on top of a volcano waiting for it to erupt. It did, in June 1967. Noel was 15. He complained of pain in his right wrist and it became swollen – but as swelling was normal with any bleed we weren't unduly suspicious. Then doubts began to creep in when it didn't show any sign of improving – but surely fate couldn't be this cruel, he'd had more than his share already. Melanie was in her first year as a student nurse at the Eye Hospital in Bristol, and when she came home on leave, she was very suspicious too. We always had a stock of painkilling tablets in, so we were able to keep him comfortable, but realised we must contact our own doctor immediately. (Some people may wonder why Noel didn't have an immediate transfusion once a bleed started – but he had been transfused so much, it was often difficult to find a vein to get the drip in – then he had to go to theatre to have a 'cut down'. It was decided he must only be transfused when really imperative.)

When our own GP saw Noel (actually it was his favourite one), there was no hesitation, a phone call was made and we were on our way once again to Southmead, and he was admitted. Same ward, same sister, same set-up and there's no other way of saying it, same diagnosis when Mr Jones looked at the X-rays. Yes, another bone-cyst. It was now just over five years since Noel's first amputation, and different techniques and new knowledge had come to the fore in the treatment of haemophilia, particularly at Oxford. The fact that this was Noel's fourth bone-cyst made him even more of a 'freak', if you like, for want of a better word.

Mr Jones, made contact with Oxford, and even larger quantities of Cryoprecipitate were administered by transfusion. Poor Noel had his drip in his left arm, and his right arm suspended up in a sling for the blood to drain as much as possible from his hand. The fingers and whole hand were becoming very swollen – and once again the pain was excruciating. He was having pethidine constantly. We naturally thought that if he had to have yet another op, Mr Jones would perform it. Imagine our distress when we were sent for and Mr Jones told us that he thought the best chance Noel had was to be transferred to the Orthopaedic Hospital at Oxford and Professor Duthey of the Haemophiliac Centre would make the decision about what to do. We felt the end of the world had come; Southmead was like a second home to Noel, we knew the staff and everyone so well there. Added to which, we knew how dreadfully upset Noel would be. God, what else could happen? Yet it had to be. As Shakespeare said, 'If it 'twere done when 'tis done, then 'twere well it was done quickly.'

Things certainly did move very quickly. Two days from when we were told, on one of the hottest days of the summer, transport was arranged. A staff nurse was to travel with us, as Noel still had a drip in. (This swung from the ceiling of the ambulance on the journey.) Melanie had obtained leave and came up with me, travelling in with Noel, with Daddy as usual following in the car. Noel was too ill to realise all that was happening.

It was the worst journey ever. Melanie was terribly upset; after all she was only 17 and was as conscious of what the probable outcome would be as I was. Noel was in a very distressed state and had to be given oxygen repeatedly. The effect of the pethidine he'd been given before leaving Southmead soon wore off.

At long, long, last we reached Oxford. Neither my husband nor I had ever been there before. What lay ahead of us and particularly Noel? How would he react to his new surroundings? What would the doctors and Professor Duthey be like? Would they be able to save his arm? The endless queries went round and round in my head, and from the look on my husband's face he was as apprehensive as I was.

So began a new era.

6

Oxford

When we entered the Nuffield Orthopaedic feeling very lost and totally bemused, to say nothing of how Noel was, it seemed like the end of the world. Then to our rescue came Mr Steele, a specialist, who had been awaiting our arrival. He immediately put us at ease and assured us that Mr David Jones had forwarded all the gen on Noel to them, and they knew what they were up against. Noel was admitted to the children's ward, and while Melanie stayed with him, my husband and I, following normal procedure, answered countless questions. (So many of them we'd answered lots of times before.) We stayed at the hospital for the rest of the day, to get Noel settled in – but when we left for home, though we knew we'd see him again the next day, we once again felt we'd deserted him.

The following day we met Professor Duthey and his team from the Haemophiliac Centre. They seemed quite hopeful that they could contain the cyst with even more massive doses of Crypo-precipitate and save his hand. His arm was again suspended in the air, this time packed in ice. Noel was in considerable pain. We'd seen it all before. Several days passed and he was transferred into a room on his own. It was unbearably hot, and Noel was sweating profusely. He was so uncomfortable with both arms immobile and the pain was yet again becoming more intense. The faces of the 'higher-ups' varied in expressions from disbelief to embarrassment. They had been so sure all would be well – but they hadn't met anyone like Noel before. Again the uncertainty continued for two weeks, with Noel getting progressively worse.

We visited him every Tuesday and Thursday and stayed each weekend in Oxford so we could be with him as much as possible.

My husband picked me up straight from school on the weekdays, and, armed with a Thermos flask (kindly prepared for me by the canteen staff) plus sandwiches etc., we belted the 70 miles up there. Both of us knew it was a losing battle – but daren't put it into words. It meant so much to him to have us there, but it was soul-destroying when we left. The nurses were wonderfully kind, and there was one doctor in particular that Noel loved, but we couldn't get up there quickly enough.

When we received a phone call asking us to go up to hear what had been decided, we dropped everything and went. It was on a Wednesday. Mr Steele was the one to give us the news. He was a very compassionate man and before he said one word, we knew from the look on his face – yes, it had become imperative to amputate. We weren't told how much they intended to remove. (I don't think they knew themselves till they actually operated.) The operation was booked for the next day.

We stayed until we were thrown out – way past the normal visiting time; we found it so very difficult to tear ourselves away. It almost seemed as if Noel realised something was up, as he kept saying, 'Don't go, Mummy.' I cried all the way home and couldn't dispel the sight of his hand with its sausage-like fingers from my mind.

We were told the operation would be in the morning and if we rang about two there should be news. Every minute of that morning seemed like an hour, yet when the time came to ring up I almost lacked the courage. But I did; the little warrior had made it yet again. I know I thanked God, yet not really knowing what for, and I prayed this would be the last of the amputations. We were asked not to go to see him on the Thursday, as he would be heavily sedated all day, but we could go any time on the Friday. We went up immediately after we'd had a bite of breakfast.

On arrival the first shock came when Noel wasn't in the children's ward or the little room he'd been in prior to his op. Then a doctor told us he'd been transferred to the men's ward, where there was a senior sister in charge who'd had extensive experience in nursing haemophiliacs. We dashed along corridors and eventually found him in a small side ward off the main one. What a shock we had. He looked absolutely ghastly. He had one drip into the ankle of his good leg and another one into the femoral vein of his 'little leg', and with all the padding and strapping on his right arm, this left him with one limb that was mobile. We knew without telling that he was desperately ill, and he remained this way and on the danger list for four weeks. He wasn't making the headway he should have done, even with continuous transfusions. Decisions had to be made again.

Finally it was decided they would have to give him a course of AHG (anti-haemophiliac globulin). Pig's blood is the nearest to human's. This vaccine can only be administered intravenously for one course, so it was very important this was written up immediately on his Haemophiliac Card. (Wherever Noel went, this card went with him.) There is a bovine vaccine which can be used in an emergency. We were there the morning he was given the pig AHG. For a time all went as it should – then he started a rigor. He shook and jerked uncontrollably and of course was giving himself more pain and was in a very fraught state. We fetched the sister, who contacted the Haemophiliac Centre and within two minutes flat a doctor came and gave him an injection to control the rigor. Soon the shaking stopped and he quietened down. He had a 20-day course of the pig vaccine – and it did the trick. Healing processes were under way. (I never particularly liked pigs but I must say I viewed them through different eyes after this experience.)

I must have said somewhere along the way that I thought Southmead Hospital was the tops, but to be strictly fair I would have to bracket the Nuffield with them as equal firsts.

The sister in the men's ward was another one in a million. I'm sure she was the one that tipped the scales for Noel. Sister Dunne became a real friend and ally to us too. Once he started to improve and was able to talk there was many a laugh. Sister Dunne was the first one to break the news to us of how much had been amputated, in the kindest possible way and with such understanding of our feelings. Later Mr Steele and Professor Duthey gave us more details. They had been able to leave the elbow joint, so Noel had a little bit of the forearm left that he would eventually be able to turn up and down. (Biscuits and sweets were often balanced on this in later years!)

It was a real red-letter day when he left the side ward and was considered well enough to go into the main ward (particularly as it boasted a television!). Noel was still flat on his back, with one drip now, but he had more to see going on around him. He really began to make strides in his recovery and the men in the ward who were up on their feet were fantastic to him. There were several other haemophiliacs in the ward and, knowing what Noel had been through and how many amputations he'd had, they realised they weren't so badly off themselves. Two of them were very mild haemophiliacs who'd never had a major bleed. The degree of haemophilia is supposed to be constant in a family but Noel's bleeding time before clotting (when tested) was considerably longer than my brother's.

We got quite friendly with one young haemophiliac and he enjoyed chatting to Melanie when she visited Noel. (He was 20.) He was very intelligent, but it soon became apparent to us that he had a big chip on his shoulder. He openly admitted his dislike for his mother, because as he said, 'It was through her I am like I am.' Sadly, she knew exactly how he felt. When she and his father visited him, which was regularly, he only chatted to his father. At least Noel knew how much we loved him and returned our love, if he did only have limited intelligence. There's always something to be thankful for.

The young man in question was discharged before Noel and he had a long conversation with us before he left. He was very frank and honest and he confessed that he hadn't taken to Noel at all at first – but as the days and weeks had gone by Noel had won his respect and admiration. This is the effect he had on people.

When we were eventually told Noel was 'out of the woods', how much happier our trips to Oxford became and the weekends were the highlight of the week. Noel's welcome on arrival was worth waiting for. We met some wonderfully kind people during Noel's stay at the Nuffield. They realised how much it was costing us each weekend to put up in Oxford and invited us to their homes for the odd meal, and several times we stayed the night. A few weekends we actually stayed in the Haemophiliac Hostel and catered for ourselves.

Fortunately for us and particularly Noel, one of our nephews had a bachelor flat in Oxford, so it was a great relief to us to know that he visited Noel at least twice a week on the nights we didn't get up there. Noel was very fond of 'Big David', as he called him. (This was because his father's name was David too – but he was much smaller!)

Noel was transferred to the Nuffield in the June of 1967 and he was still there for his birthday on September 23rd – so he had his sixteenth birthday there. That was a day to remember. He was king for a day! By this time he was well on the way to recovery, though his little arm was still well cocooned and he couldn't sit up on his own. All the men in the ward had collected to buy him a present, a cake had been baked at the hospital, and of course Mel, his Daddy and I had gone up with many other gifts from friends at home as well as ours. One of his presents was a mouth-organ. (He'd always loved musical toys and had had one years before – but it had got lost somehow.) He was so thrilled to have one again and immediately 'played' a little tune. Amazingly enough, although it was his own tune it was never discordant. His darling sister told him he could play it – so it was all in order. The other patients in the ward told us they could always tell how Noel was feeling by his 'tunes'. Often they were rather plaintive, but as he continued to progress they became very lively! Apparently the doctors asked him for a tune when their rounds were completed!

Every Sunday there was a service in the ward taken by a local vicar, who used to ask for favourite hymns from the patients. Noel's choice never varied from 'All things bright and beautiful' and 'We plough the fields and scatter'. (These he loved all through his school days.) On the Sundays these were chosen we all joined in with gusto, but Daddy was a bit of a back-slider and Noel had to keep him up to the mark with, 'you must sing, Daddy. Sister said!' This wasn't said in dulcet tones either!

His favourite song was 'Oh, What a Beautiful Morning'. Uncle Bert had sung this to him from a very early age. We never knew who instigated the following – staff or patients – but one morning on a request programme for hospitals, Noel's name was read out and there was a rendering of said song. He naturally joined in with the bits he knew in his usual 'teddy-bear' voice!

As we had found so many times, after the dreadful days there invariably came a lull in the storm, and with continued improvement in his condition we knew we must be on the homeward stretch. There was one set-back however, but not a serious one. He had a bleed into the neck muscles, which meant more Cryoprecipitate, but this resolved itself in about a week and once again we were wondering when he'd be discharged. Inexorably the day did come (Noel was never told he was actually coming out till the morning of the day, in case of snags.) What jubilation when he did know! and oh how many 'good-byes', 'good lucks', and kisses were exchanged!

The journey home was opposite in every way from the one up. It was a lovely day and as it was now early autumn there was no oppressive heat. We seemed to virtually fly home. Noel was so excited and kept asking every few miles, 'Where's my house?' His 'little arm' now only had light protective dressings on, and amazingly enough he'd never asked any questions about it. (No doubt they would come later.) The ambulance men were two super fellows who really entered into the spirit of the occasion. It did pass through my mind, I wonder if we'll ever do this journey again? My husband had kept a record of the miles we'd done over the four months and it amounted to 9,000!

Once Noel was home he was under the care of our own doctor, who was exceptionally understanding, and all went well. It was many months though before he used his 'little arm' to hold things down, to conduct music on the telly and to once more fold the washing! It was such a help when he was able to dig his little arm in to get up in bed, on his own. I suppose it was a small advantage that his amputations were opposite sides of his body, from the balance point of view. With all that had happened at Oxford, and all he'd endured, we'd made lots of new friends, and made contact with different medical people. We had been told that any bleeds Southmead couldn't cope with, they would always have Noel at Oxford.

I can say now that thankfully he never had any more amputations, but he did have two more periods in the Nuffield Orthopaedic. The next one came early in 1970. He was admitted into the same ward, and fortunately for him Sister Dunne was still in charge of Randle Ward. He was again under Mr Steel and

Professor Duthey. Noel had had a massive bleed into the thigh of his good leg, and with all the transfusions he'd had at Southmead they hadn't stopped the bleed. His thigh was colossal and rock hard. Mr Jones made the decision once more to transfer him to the Nuffield.

The journey to Oxford was again traumatic. We saw the top of the Cotswolds now in winter. A very different scene from the summer and autumn ones we'd seen so often. During our usual pattern of trips up, we got used to different landmarks. A farm with a rather appropriate name stands out in my memory, Cold Comfort Farm – it certainly looked it! A village down in a hollow that both my husband and I thought looked rather spooky and medieval even in the summertime, looked positively eerie in the winter and like something out of another world. I was always glad to leave it behind. Then there were the pubs we didn't have time to stop at on the way up and they were usually closed on our way back!

We were determined to keep up our pattern of visiting Noel because we knew how much it meant to him, but the winter journeys weren't as easy to cope with as the earlier ones. Lots of nights we encountered thick fog and icy patches, and arrived home shattered, particularly my husband as he had to do all the driving.

Imagine our consternation waking up one Tuesday morning to find the outer world covered with snow – and this on a day when we were due to visit Noel in the evening. It would be bad enough getting to our places of work – but whatever would it be like on the top of the Cotswolds? It was bound to be worse there. What to do? I waited until the afternoon then rang the AA to see if there was any chance of us getting through. They gave us a 50–50 chance, but advised against it. Crickley Hill, which we had to go up, they said was particularly hazardous. I got in touch with my husband and he thought it was quite ridiculous to even attempt it, but being me, I had no intention of being beaten and I stuck to my guns, and we went!

That was a journey to remember – slithering, sliding, sinking, bumping over snow ruts, but ever moving onwards, all accompanied by recriminations from my husband that he'd always thought I was mad and now he knew! We did make it, but an hour and a half late. (Fortunately Noel couldn't see the clock from his bed, else he would have been upset, thinking we weren't coming.)

We were greeted by such a cheer when we arrived in the ward from all the patients well enough to give us one – and Noel's face was reward in itself. One of the men patients had been taking bets as to whether we'd make it or not and was pleased to tell us he'd won money on us! We didn't stay our usual length of time that evening – but it was long enough for us to make contact with Noel, give him love, and perhaps help him, through our strength. Though the homeward journey was even worse for us, it had been well worth while.

Unfortunately during this stay at the Nuffield, on top of all the other pain, transfusions and trauma he had renal failure. It really was incredible what Noel survived. The other patients were amazed when he started to improve and they realised what a different person Noel was when free from pain. While visiting, we became quite involved with another patient in the ward. He was probably in his early thirties and he too was in severe pain – yet showed great concern over Noel. Fortunately he was able to have an operation on his spine which was very successful. After his op, we had many conversations with him. (This was usually when Melanie had come up with us – so Noel still had two visitors while one of us chatted to Jim.) I think he was so relieved that he was going to be fine himself that he wanted to do something for us, as every time we went up he wanted to treat us to a meal out! While thanking him for this gesture, I finally convinced him we weren't really short of money as I was working as well as my husband. When he kept on insisting I eventually said 'If you want to do something worthwhile, give a donation to the Haemophiliac Society.' On our next visit up he called us over and gave me a cheque for £25 for the Society. I was really taken aback. He was discharged before Noel, but a couple of months later we received a parcel from him. It contained the book *Nicholas and Alexandra* (this is the story of the Russian Royal Family and the haemophilia running through it) and a very charming letter saying how often he thought of Noel and us.

Oddly enough, Noel's last stay at the Nuffield was at the end of 1970 – again for a bleed but into the other thigh. This time, still in Randle Ward and with Sister Dunne, he was only in for a month. He made exceptionally good progress – probably because it wasn't such a massive bleed. (No two were ever alike.) Wherever Noel went he had his favourites and his favourite doctor at Oxford was a Dr Matthews. He was a saint, so gentle, and was able to do anything with Noel. We could never forget him or all the others who brought Noel back from the brink so many times.

7

Southmead – Revisited

After Noel's arm amputation, when he'd been put in the men's ward at Oxford, we wondered how he'd react to the children's ward again at Southmead. (We knew it was on the cards he'd have to be re-admitted there some time or other.) Actually, it had been decided at Southmead that as Noel was then 16 in the future he would go to E Ward – one of the men's wards. So it would be another change-over for him. Goodbye to Tall Kister and his other darlings. We too wondered how we were going to get on with yet another sister and a new set-up. Inevitably Noel did get a bad bleed which needed hospital treatment and he made his first journey to E Ward. Almost in fear and trepidation we went to the office to see the sister. Imagine our surprise when 'she' turned out to be a man! It would be impossible to forget how wonderful he was with Noel. He was a tall, bluff man with a hearty laugh who inspired confidence. Noel took to him straight away like a duck to water. His name was Ricketts but Noel called him 'Mr Cricket'.

He was a perfectionist, and by God his ward was well run. Everyone pulled his or her weight, but he was extremely fair and respected by all. Over the years he saved our sanity many a time. He allowed us to go in whenever convenient to us and he informed the nursing staff we were permitted to wash and deal with Noel's bodily functions in the way we did at home, because we knew more about him than they did! (Noel wasn't able to sit on bed-pans because of starting bleeds. We'd evolved our own system – which worked well!) Being fair-skinned, he only needed shaving every other day so my husband did this when we went down in the evening. The biggest blessing about Southmead was that we could see him every day.

During Mr Ricketts' 'reign' so many things happened that will live with us for ever. We learnt a lot about life and people along the way, and that appearances can often be misleading. This is one incident that proved the point. Noel had been rushed down early one evening once again requiring immediate transfusions. We stayed with him to keep him as calm as possible while 'they' endeavoured to find a vein to put the drip in. After an hour and X number of doctors had had a go, Noel was over the top – and we were nearly the same.

A surgeon was brought in who had just done an emergency op. Quite frankly he looked like a Rugby player, but he handled Noel like gossamer and said, 'He's had enough, take him up to theatre for a cut down.'

So we waited for the stretcher to take him. In less than no time, into the ward came the two stretcher bearers. What a contrast to each other they were. Leading the way was Mr Efficiency plus, all bustle and self-assurance (a man about 40) and bringing up the rear was a loose-limbed, long-haired youth, rather unkept but with a very friendly smile. Noel was by this time beside himself and in a terrible state. When Mr Efficiency began to remove him from the bed on to the stretcher the balloon went up and he was screaming uncontrollably. To our utter amazement, the youth took over and asked the older man to give him a few minutes with Noel. He did just that – talking calmly and soothingly, holding his hand and reassuring him. Although Noel was still very distraught, he allowed them, without struggling, to put him on the stretcher. Once again he was on his way to theatre to be attached to his life-line. We went up in the lift with them and when we had a chance expressed our gratitude to the young man. He smiled, shrugged, and said he was only doing his job, but we knew he was something rather special. One more battle had been won.

It was during this sojourn in E Ward that a Chinese youth was admitted and put in the bed opposite Noel. He couldn't speak a word of English. He had been brought in from a boat that had docked at Avonmouth. Communication between him and the medical staff was nil, and they were getting nowhere fast. Fortunately someone remembered there was a Chinese nurse in another part of the hospital. As luck would have it, she was on duty at the time and was brought post-haste to E Ward. Things went much more easily after that. She explained to him (we were told later) that he had to have an operation for appendicitis and this was performed the same evening. When he was beginning to improve it was very noticeable that he was interested in Noel – and Noel seemed fascinated by him. As soon as the Chinese lad could walk, he spent all his time by Noel's bedside. While neither of them understood a word the other was saying, they found pleasure in each other's company and grinned from ear to ear. Noel, too, was improving all the time and it was lovely to hear them laugh together.

There was one very special friend Noel had in E Ward and that was Nurse Webb. She was like a second mother to him and, as she was permanently attached to the ward, she and Mr Ricketts worked wonderfully well together. She, too, was another unique person – who gave her all to her job and nothing was too much trouble. We always felt happier on leaving Noel if Nurse Webb and Mr Ricketts were on duty. We slept better those nights! We saw Nurse Webb off and on for many years and admired her even more as time went on. We owed her so much. On one occasion Noel was in E Ward at the same time as his Uncle Bert. When he was improving once more, they were put near each other and Noel was highly delighted.

One Christmas Melanie gave Noel a large ventriloquist's dummy – a boy in a check suit and cap, with ginger hair. There's no question about it, but of all the toys Noel ever had 'Charlie Cooper', as he christened him, was his favourite – and remained so for the rest of his life. After the loss of his 'Aunty pillow' he was allowed to take Charlie into hospital when he was admitted. Charlie had the privilege of sitting on Noel's locker and I had the job of performing with him when Noel was well enough to enjoy it! (I became so expert that many of my friends said I'd missed my vocation!) Charlie, however, once fell out of a second-storey window at Southmead Hospital (all the patients had been transferred to another ward due to decorating). Believe me, until he was retrieved there was panic stations! Charlie had been put on the window ledge while the locker was tidied.

Unwittingly, Charlie was the cause of an elderly gentleman

getting a bit of a shock. He (the patient) confided to us one evening that when he was coming round from his op he couldn't understand why there was a little man sitting on the locker opposite him! He also admitted that he was very relieved when he found out what or who Charlie was! The nurses, some of the doctors and of course Mr Cricket always found time to have a few words with Charlie, and when Noel was discharged, Charlie received almost as many good-byes as he did! Anything that brought a bit of light relief into his life was well worth while.

With all his suffering, Noel was very fortunate in having so many people who cared for him, not for just a short period but for many years. Tall Kister from the children's ward, as soon as she heard on the hospital grapevine that Noel was in, was usually one of the first to visit him in E Ward. Noel's greeting to her varied between 'Oh, my darling Tall Kister' and 'I'm a poor old man, me very ill' – depending on how he felt. More often than not he was past talking at all by the time he reached hospital, but she always sat by him and held his hand for a while. She had been such a tower of strength to him. In later years she left the nursing side and went into administration, so we didn't see as much of her. Personally, I think it was a mistake and I believe she had second thoughts too.

There was always one person who brought some light relief to Noel when he was on the mend. This was a nursing tutor, a man, who came to see him and invariably gave a rendering of 'Hello Dolly'. Noel complimented him with 'You very good Uncle!'.

It's amazing really how a simple mistake or misunderstanding can completely change a situation. It happened to us in this way. Yet again Noel had been rushed down to E Ward with a major bleed and this time there wasn't one single person there who knew him. There had been a change-over of doctors, Nurse Webb and Mr Ricketts were on holiday and nothing seemed to drop into place. We were asked who Noel was under and of course said Mr Jones. Eventually Noel's notes were produced (a veritable tome) and the usual pattern was followed. Imagine our surprise when we visited the next day to find he had the name Dr Verrier Jones on the top of his bed. We immediately went to see the relief sister (again a man) and explained that a mistake had been made. We didn't like this young man very much; it was mutual it seemed, but when we got to know each other better and he realised what a difficult case Noel was, all was well.

Dr Verrier Jones saw us the next day, and said though a mistake had been made, it would probably be better for Noel to be under him, as of course lots of his bleeds were nothing to do with the orthopaedic side. He assured us he would look after Noel for us and could always contact Mr David Jones when necessary. He kept his word. Many, many times he earned our gratitude and, most important of all Noel took to him. He always found time to explain what was going on and what difficulties they were encountering and how they hoped to combat them. We were never left out of the picture. On several occasions he even rang me at school to ask for our opinion. He knew he could always depend on us to co-operate in any way we could if it was for Noel's good; and we had complete confidence in him. Dr Verrier Jones looked after Noel for many years, but Mr David Jones kept in touch and often popped in to see him.

So the years went on, and as Noel's general condition worsened he was confined more and more to bed. Then another problem reared its head. Because of all the transfusions Noel had had he'd developed lots of antibodies in his blood. This made the cross-matching even more difficult. On several occasions blood was flown in for him by helicopter from other blood banks.

Eventually Dr Verrier Jones sent for us and told us he thought Noel had developed Australian antigen and his liver was affected (due to the countless transfusions) and in future unless the bleed was an extremely dangerous one they would try to avoid transfusing and just sedate him and administer pain killers with no hospitalisation if possible. We were, however, positively assured there would always be a bed for Noel at Southmead in any emergency.

Now the cards were on the table and we knew that we would have more to cope with at home than ever before. This situation would mean covering the nights as well as the days for long periods and with both of us doing a full-time job it was going to be tough. Yet somehow we did manage, though it left its mark on us. In our thirties and forties it wasn't too bad to miss out on a few nights' sleep – but in our fifties we were beginning to feel the strain and it showed. When Noel was in a bad patch with a bleed, this was our sleep pattern. The first week my husband and I alternated between one night in bed, and then one up with Noel, maybe if we were lucky getting the odd cat-nap in. The next week we did a split shift from 10–2 and 2–7. (My husband usually did the first one and mine was the latter part of the night; I had the dawn chorus one and waiting for a new day to start.) If he was in a pretty bad way we both stayed down with him – as moral support for each other! The two weeks were repeated till all was well.

Over the years we 'slept' on a rather wide range of things from a mattress on the floor, the settee, camp beds (murder for dodgy backs), cushions and eventually graduated to a double bed put-u-up which seemed the epitome of luxury to drop down on when Noel was in a quiet phase. It wasn't only the physical side which drained us, it was the mental – the constant worry of what was coming next, and the effort required to be on top of our jobs as well.

I tried so hard not to let any of my home worries rear their heads in front of my class – but there are always the perceptive children. One instance stands out so much in my mind. (We had had a particularly bad patch with Noel and I'd felt as taut as a violin string.) My class, nine-year-olds, were having indoor games in the hall. We were playing dodge-ball and we were left with one boy in the middle whom we couldn't get out. He was leaping round like a performing flea and the rest were in fits of laughter. Eventually it got to me too and I succumbed and laughed uproariously. Then I felt a hand slipped in mine and a girl's voice said, 'Mrs Swann, you laughed.' I stopped in amazement and asked 'What do you mean, Helen? Is it so rare for me to laugh?' To which she replied, 'You haven't laughed like that for weeks.' I've thought so many times of that child – I hope life won't treat her harshly.

Our GPs were exceptionally good to us during the years Noel didn't have so many trips to hospital; we kept an excellent stock of pain-relievers always at hand, but essentially there were the times he had to be admitted. During this period he was rushed in, again in the middle of the night, to Southmead with a massive bleed into the scrotum. He was in extreme pain. He landed up in a surgical ward, instead of his usual 'E', and the registrar who attended him was yet another Dr Jones! On this occasion Noel was vomiting pethidine back and Dr Jones came up with the idea of using pain killers in pessary form into the rectum. (He had never had these before.) They were wonderful and after his discharge we always had a supply of these, used under our GP's guidance) of course. (One of these pessaries was the last 'help' Noel received on this earth.)

Of course I haven't recorded every bleed or every trip to hospital Noel made – how could I? It would have been quite impossible – but I've covered the major ones and I think given a pretty fair cross-section of what he had to endure. Yet with it all he had his happy moments as you will see in the following chapters.

8

Food and Drink

As with all invalids and people not able to lead a full and active life, food played a tremendously important part in Noel's existence.

When he was well, he had a very good appetite but strong views on what he liked and disliked! On reflecting what a problem it was to get him to suckle and eat during his earlier years, he certainly made up for it later on, but many of his dislikes lasted throughout his lifetime. We never managed to persuade him to eat apples or oranges or even just taste them, and only bananas if mashed up with sugar. Fortunately he adored cabbage and all green vegetables (except broad beans) so got his Vitamin C that way. Runner beans, an especial favourite, were called 'funny beans'. For many years he insisted on baked beans on toast for lunch – then suddenly for no reason at all it was 'No more beans on toast' and that was that. He never touched them again.

Only once he tasted an egg and was immediately sick – so that was something else ruled out. There is no question at all his favourite meal of the day was his evening meal. As he got older and was confined to bed he took even more interest in his food and what he was going to have and I had to tell him in advance the menu for every day of the week. This would be relayed back to me each morning, often accompanied by rubbing his tummy if it happened to be one of his favourites! He much preferred savoury food to sweet, adoring Marmite in preference to jam etc. Cakes and puddings were sheer anathema to him so he never tasted Christmas cake or pud. He always had a birthday cake – but this to him meant just blowing candles out! Ice-cream he adored, but we kept this to the minimum because of the fat content.

During the latter years of his life, I suppose his days revolved round his meal-times. He very much liked routine and things happening at the same time each day. Even 'coffee time' for More Aunty and Top Cat had to be precisely on the dot of 10 o'clock. When he was able to he coped with his own drink using flexi-straws (another firm we must have kept in business) and his biscuit he balanced on the end of his 'little arm'. (This was one of his party pieces!)

It was so nice when Noel had been able to feed himself, but for many years before he died his elbow joints on his good arm had become so fixed it was an impossibility. Daddy usually gave him his main meal on weekdays, while watching *Crossroads* at the same time! Having had the arm amputation did create lots of problems, as when his good arm had a bleed he was left with virtually nothing. Our meal times became very prolonged and my husband and I seldom had a meal together.

Noel adored all kinds of meat and one of his firm favourites was 'pork sausages'. Chicken was christened 'cock-cock' meat, while turkey was 'big cock-cock'! Liver was 'limma', and beef was just 'very lovely meat'.

When he was young he was very partial to fish – but we were always scared stiff he'd swallow a bone. We did have a couple of scares, but with no desperate after-effects. However, after one visit to hospital on returning home he wouldn't even look at fish. We often wondered and never found out what had put him off.

Like all children (and some adults) he was absolutely 'gone' on chips, and would have eaten them with everything if he'd been given the chance! He never quite mastered the difference between ham and lamb – but knew he had mint sauce, which he thought was super, with one of them. Stew was always greeted with great enthusiasm by Noel – but not so much by Daddy, as Noel always insisted on eating things in it in strict rotation. (This was in the days when he had to be fed.) Woe betide if he was proffered something in the wrong order!

When young, Melanie and Noel often had a combined birthday party as their birthdays were so close together. One year it was held on Mel's actual day and the next on Noel's. I still have a vivid memory of the year Noel disgraced himself (he was probably five or six) when he visited the room where the repast lay before anyone else and scoffed all the sausages on sticks. He had enough intelligence to leave the sticks, but not enough to hide them. There they lay in a pathetic heap on the plate! Mel was on the verge of tears, when one of the other children invited started to giggle and said, 'Let's count the sticks, then we'll know how many he's had!' So it ended up with us all laughing. The little blighter didn't even have a twinge of pain after that episode and slept the night through peacefully!

Cheese was another firm favourite in any form, but roasted on toast with tomato sauce was probably the best loved. Cauliflower cheese came a close second! There were a few things Noel ate in hospital that he wouldn't eat at home. Custard was one of them. I never found out why their custard was nicer than mine. Mashed potatoes were refused at home but eaten in hospital. He adored gravy and would never leave a drop – but one up to me, he thought hospital gravy 'very terrible'.

When it came to drinks, Noel wouldn't touch tea, coffee or cocoa, so apart from soft drinks he either had milk, or milk and hot water, (half and half) or water when ill. He regarded it as a very special treat when he had a weak cider-shandy in his 'grown-up' years. There was much lip-smacking over this. At Christmas time or birthdays we allowed him a very, very small sherry. There was lots of 'cheers' and glass raising on these occasions.

He had his first drink of whisky at the age of six! I think the years five to nine were his most mischievous. Two cousins of mine had arrived unexpectedly on a very cold wintry day and having decided they needed something to warm them up – the whisky bottle had been fetched out. The glasses were put on a tray and filled in readiness to hand round. For some reason or other, there was a slight delay in this procedure and then to our horror we saw Noel gasping for breath and getting redder and redder in the face. On looking at the tray we noticed that one glass now stood innocently empty! The speed at which he'd taken it was almost unbelievable. We were a bit foxed about what to do – whether to make him sick or just leave it in the lap of the gods. We decided on the latter. When he got his breath back the first words were 'Very lubbly Mummy!' Amazingly enough there were no dreadful effects – but he did sleep for 12 hours solidly afterwards and then woke up as bright as a button!

From a very early age we had to clamp down on Noel over sweets, and by and large he was exceptionally good over this. Mainly our concern was for his teeth. He would have what we gave him and accepted it when we refused. Even when he was older and had a box of chocolates at birthdays and Christmas on his bed, he always asked before having one and then they had to be handed round. Biscuits, though, were another concern. He was mad on them. I used to tell Top Cat and More Aunty, he must not have more than two at coffee-time but he always tried it on, to get more – sometimes succeeding!

Noel was always very interested when we were stocking up the deep freeze. (The freezer room was next to his, so everything passed through.) We had to tell him in detail what was in each bag and comments varied between, 'Very terrible' – with a grimace (that was fish) – to 'that's better, me like that, very super grub!' Daddy's answer to 'What's that?' was usually, 'Food for your fat tummy, Noel' – to which he would chuckle and rub his midriff! This ritual never varied.

The very last Sunday dinner he ate before he died on the Wednesday, he thoroughly enjoyed and as was his norm said, 'Very nice dinner, Mummy.' It so happened it was one of his favourites. Not being able to sound his r's, it was woast beef, funny beans, woast potatoes and gwavy! It was very, very seldom he had pudding. A good thing too, as he easily put on weight and was quite chubby. This didn't quite tie in with his statement when hungry, 'Me starving.' He certainly never looked it.

Noel loved it when we had visitors and I put on a spread. He always called it a 'tea party' and joined in with gusto. Best of all was when it was a help yourself do and we ate in his room – but when it was a sit-down meal, by leaving his door wide open he was able to see us and not feel left out, and of course Daddy or I fed him.

The last Christmas he was alive, Melanie issued an ultimatum and said Daddy and I had to have our Christmas dinner together for once and she would feed Noel. After much demurring we agreed and the meal was voted a great success by all – but Noel kept saying to Mel, 'You will have yours after!' It was a very happy Christmas.

I love to remember how he enjoyed his meals when well. One has to eat to live, but Noel virtually lived to eat! This is the poem Mel wrote at the end of that Christmas.

> This is the nicest Xmas that we've ever had,
> We've stuffed ourselves with turkey and salad.
> Roast potatoes, sausages and beans,
> Pork and stuffing, curly greens.
> Xmas pudding, custard too,
> Cheese and biscuits, lots of goo!
> Mints and wine (a posh affair)
> All the best of table ware.
> Stomachs full and most replete
> We stagger to a comfy seat.
> 'Dad make some tea for us' says Mum
> Or, if you'd rather, have a rum!
> Noel sits with nose glued to the 'Tele'
> Still wanting food inside his belly!

9

Toys and Entertainment

By about the age of four Noel was getting quite good at keeping himself amused provided he had a varied selection of things around him. There were the odd occasions though when we had to scratch our heads to think of something different to hold his interest. Definitely by this time we recognised his brand of humour, as the odd rather infectious chuckle emerged, which in later years developed into quite a rumbustious laugh. Even when happily engaged in playing, though, he needed people and checked regularly where I or Daddy was or whoever was in charge. He could never have been described as a loner.

All the toys Noel had were strictly vetted for rough or sharp edges and didn't have to be too large for him to handle. Winding up ones always fascinated him, and humming tops. (Melanie usually got the tops going.) His favourite possession without any doubt was his ball – it never left him! But Noel's passion for balls almost caused a tragedy. During his early years he lay on a sofa when ill in the living room. The incident I am about to relate happened when he was about two and a half, so Mel would have been four and a half. He was getting better from a bleed into his leg, but still had to lie up on the sofa and was being a bit fractious. To help amuse him we came up with the idea of putting a ball in a nylon stocking and suspending it from the beam above his head. He was able to swing this about and derive pleasure from doing it. Unfortunately our good idea misfired. For some completely unknown reason, Melanie stood on the sofa and twisted the stocking (with the ball at the end) round and round her neck then jumped off! Fortunately for Mel, her grandad walked into the room at that moment (her feet were off the floor and she was choking). He was able to support her and unwind the stocking. She was a very frightened little girl. She could never give an explanation of why she'd done it other than she thought it would make Noel laugh. It horrified my husband and myself to think what might have happened; and it would have been our fault. The stocking and ball were removed from the beam and never, ever went up again.

As Noel grew older we found it easier to get toys which he could enjoy and yet had an educational value as well. He had a frame with large coloured beads, and snap cards and the normal pack of playing cards he loved. There was usually someone available to give him a game, but if not he enjoyed sorting them out. Happy family cards fell into this category too. By the time he went to school he was able to do simple jigsaw puzzles. It always amazed me how often I came across backward children who were able to do jigsaw puzzles better than children with a much higher IQ.

Plasticene was a wonderful substance for him to have fun with, and the animals he made – pig, dog, cat etc. – although looking all the same, at least had the requisite number of legs, ears and heads! It was the same with pastry. On my cooking days, like all children, and under Mel's supervision, he rolled and cut out countless fancy shapes. (Again I checked the cutters for sharp edges.)

Noel must have been quite 12 before he realised what winning and losing was all about. He finally cottoned on after we'd played countless games of snakes and ladders. He loved this pursuit and learnt a lot along the way. At first we counted the spots on the dice – but eventually he recognised the number by the way the dots were arranged. I'd love a pound for every game we played, at home and in hospital! He never wanted the game to finish and as he got older would cheat abominably to delay the end.

He seemed to have phases of doing different things – but one phase which outlasted all the others was colouring. He got through endless colouring books, on all different subjects – zoo, farm, school, circus, etc. – and countless crayons and felt-tips. Unfortunately we had to clamp down on too much of this as the continuous movement so often started a bleed into the wrist, elbow or fingers. Once Noel had made up his mind to do something it wasn't always easy to divert him! A nice peaceful pastime that never brought any ill-effects and he always enjoyed was blowing bubbles Mel used to join him in this pursuit to see who could blow the biggest one.

'Fuzzy Felts' were absolutely ideal for Noel and again we went through the whole range, but his favourites were the hospital and the different shaped pieces from which he could make patterns. He was very adept at this. With mosaics, too, he showed his aptitude for design. When he'd completed one we were always asked for our approval.

Noel didn't have many years of being able to play out of doors, and of course it was always spasmodic depending on his health. However, when he was able, he loved to be outside, and as we were fortunate in having a large garden, he was able to play with the inevitable sand and water. He enjoyed watching the chickens too and liked to torment the cockerel by poking sticks through the wire! In his good patches he was a typical mischievous boy, perhaps even more so – as most mongols are. Very occasionally he had a go on Mel's small three-wheeler bike – but he wasn't very keen and we certainly didn't encourage it. The swing too was rather risky, but Melanie was very protective with him and only pushed gently.

He spent many hours cutting out pictures from catalogues and glossy magazines. Even during the summer he would sit out on the lawn and, armed with a pair of rounded-ended scissors and two boxes, one for the bits and the other for his pictures he would be quite content. We still needed to watch out for pressure bruising from the scissors. He treasured his cut-outs and kept them all very tidily and no way was I allowed to get rid of any of them. There were many boxes, from over the years, still full of his pictures when he died.

In a spare bedroom we had table tennis set-up, and although Noel never understood the rules or scoring, he had great fun playing against Mel, Daddy or me – and proved yet again his love of ball games.

One Christmas we bought Noel a Scalextric and laid it out all over our living-room floor near his bed, so he could control a car from there. Sadly for Noel he started a bad bleed on the Christmas

Day and had to be rushed into hospital – so he didn't play with it at all. We took it up into the spare bedroom and laid it out there and when he came home he had lots of fun with it. This helped him too in regard to winning and losing – but he loved being able to say, 'Me won.'

Of all the things he had to help him pass his time as happily as possible, I would have to put Lego as the ultimate tops. Even after he'd had his arm amputation he managed to build and create things that were quite unbelievable with his one hand. Over the years with all the different packs he'd had he'd accumulated a very sizeable collection. (I'm pleased to relate that Noel's Lego is still being used and giving pleasure to my great-nephew.)

One of the first presents Melanie ever gave him was a fish-bowl with two goldfish in. (Noel gave them their names, Bill and Ben, from the flowerpot men programme.) He loved them and spent lots of time watching them and was terribly upset when they died. Ben got stuck up a shell, and Bill died from over-eating! Noel sometimes gave them extra food without my knowing. I only found out from the level in the cartons or odd suspicious trails. Amazingly enough, they survived quite a few years.

When Noel was unable to attend school at all, it became quite a problem to occupy and entertain him. Luckily, being in the educational field myself I was able to get puzzles and self-corrective pieces of apparatus for him. For quite a long period I continued the Janet and John reading scheme but had to discontinue this when I found he was getting distressed if he couldn't manage a word. As I was only able to do this off and on depending on his physical condition, I didn't think it fair to pressurise him. He never forgot the words he'd learnt – but I felt enough was enough. He was so apologetic and used to say, 'Very sorry, Mummy, too hard.' So we concentrated all we could on his speech. Rs and the 'sh' sound were always a problem. Thankfully, he was able to talk enough to hold a simple conversation and to tell us what he wanted etc.

A toy telephone he'd had when about seven proved to be a valuable aid when encouraging him to talk. He would use the word 'I' when practising with me but nine times out of ten reverted to 'me' when chattering or excited. Oddly enough, when telling me he was poorly he'd say 'I'm not very well.' We had lots of fun together saying words into a mirror. We also found that finger and glove puppets played a very important part in helping Noel's speech. He would talk to them and I answered. These eventually led to larger ventriloquist's dummies. Mel again was the instigator. (As previously mentioned, the first one was Charlie Cooper.) Till the day he died Noel still thought Charlie Cooper could speak!

But we didn't finish with Charlie Cooper did we? Oh no! Mel's next masterpiece was Big Bird from Sesame Street so naturally I had to find a new voice to use for him. His next birthday Kermit Frog of the Muppets fame came to reside with us! I must confess my throat reacted a little harshly to this one. From the very first day he had him, Noel decided Kermit Frog was going to be the naughty one in his collection. It always remained that way.

In fact, when our Canon (the man with the collar) retired and a new one came to visit Noel he couldn't tell him quickly enough that Kermit Frog had said SH-IT (that's how he pronounced it) to his Melanie! Top Cat, who was looking after Noel on the day of visit, knew what he was going to say and every time he got to the SH- part coughed loudly, but Noel pressed on regardless, till the Vicar got the message!

The few swear words he used always sounded somehow innocent coming from him. One of his favourite expressions was 'me fed up with the bloody weather!' I quite often went along with him on this topic!

The last one to join his gang of puppets was 'Little Owl' and I then said very firmly – no more! This one was greeted with, 'Tu whit to wu – I love you' – and Noel really did love him, often having him tucked into his 'little arm'. We've kept Little Owl.

During Noel's immobile years he kept all his treasures and favourite toys, books, puzzles etc. on a large shelf near his bed, and periodically he would say, 'Me tidy up, Mummy,' and everything had an airing, before it was all put back meticulously (sometimes requiring a little aid from me). On these occasions I was told where they 'lived'.

When people knock TV as being a time-waster and mostly rubbish – I must say I see red. To the handicapped and bed-ridden it's a life-saver. I'm quite sure our TV set must have been on more hours than anyone's in the country. Apart from the children's programmes he loved, Noel learnt so much from it.

He was a true Royalist, recognising the Queen, Queen Mother, Prince Charles, Princess Anne and Princess Margaret but Prince Philip was 'the Queen's daddy!?' When the National Anthem was played Noel insisted his daddy stood to attention and saluted. (Not always appreciated by Daddy. For some reason I was excused.)

I remember so well, the day I arrived home from school at the precise moment it was being announced Mrs Thatcher had become leader of the Conservative Party. In my usual ebullient way I leapt around in delight saying, 'Up the women,' and feeling chuffed as I'd won a bet on Mrs T's victory. For ever afterwards, when Mrs T appeared on the telly, whatever the occasion, Noel shouted 'Up the women,' and laughed like a drain! Mr Wilson he dubbed 'a good man' (his own judgement).

We generally allowed Noel to have the programmes he liked – after all he had so few pleasures in life, compared with a normal person. Mainly he viewed ITV – so he became quite well versed in the musical advertisements. The Tetley tea-bags men were regarded as 'the tops' and when they arrived on the screen, Daddy and I also had to execute their dance. Daddy usually got told off for not doing it properly – dancing not being one of his most successful attributes. The soap and detergent adverts also appealed to Noel. He liked the mild green Fairy Liquid one – but he called it Fairy wee-wee! We still do!

All adverts connected with food were always greeted enthusiastically – I wonder why? During the years he'd liked baked beans, the adverts relating to these were accompanied by 'Ooh, me like those very lubbly;' but after he'd gone off them, the expression of disgust on his face and the words 'very terrible, Mummy' never varied! The Clarkes children's shoes one in which a little girl looked very mischievous and quoted, 'Mummy said I'm a proper little madam,' tickled Noel pink, but we slipped back to reality when, looking at the pairs of shoes, his next comment was, 'Me only got one foot.' Lots of the adverts led to him exclaiming, 'I want one of those' but when this followed the Penguin chocolate one, there was just no hope of him having one.

(He wanted a real one!) He'd always been fascinated by the penguins in the zoo. Throughout his life-time Noel had been car mad, so the car and petrol ads gave him great pleasure – especially the one with the 'tiger in the tank'. He was able to pick our own car out in Daddy's motor books – and was very excited when he saw one the same on TV.

Of course the adverts didn't mean as much to him as his favourite programmes, but because they were repeated so often they too formed a part of his day and life.

The regular TV series that gave Noel his greatest pleasure were *Coronation Street* and *Crossroads*. His week revolved round these, Elsie Tanner and Meg Richardson being his 'darlings'. It was rather sad that the last few weeks of his life ITV were on strike and he kept saying, 'I will see Annie Walker again' – but he didn't. Noel reacted very much to atmosphere and was quick to sense sadness and happiness. He didn't like it when his darling Meg was sad but he thought it great when Elsie Tanner was 'very mad' and old 'Mr 'Atlock' was grumpy and in a temper. The weddings in *Coronation Street* were followed by the comment, 'All happy now.'

Westerns and car chases he followed avidly, always knowing the goodies from the baddies – often warning the 'goody' to be careful, that the bad man was behind the door, rock, etc. – and rejoicing greatly when all the terrible Indians were dead. When funerals took place he wanted to know who was 'in the box', then commented, 'No come back no more!'

It never ceased to amaze us how he recognised actors and actresses playing entirely different parts and in very varied attire. Quite frequently this happened before we'd spotted them. He had his favourite comedians and at the very top of the list came Tommy Cooper, closely followed by Morecombe and Wise and Benny Hill (Velly funny man, Mummy!) Noel really added to the enjoyment of any programme when he was well – probably because he became so involved and engrossed in it. When he wasn't interested in his telly we knew something was in the offing.

At the last General Election we stayed up till the early hours of the morning to know the result and Noel watched right through with us – resisting sleep as long as the telly was on! (We said he ought to be called 'Square eyes' after that episode.)

The school programmes during term-time helped him tremendously. He gleaned the odd bits and simply adored the nature ones. We had the first colour TV set in the district (simply because of Noel) and he was absolutely fascinated by it, but played up rotten when the odd black and white programme cropped up. He thought we could control the situation. Electricity cuts played havoc in our house other than the normal frustrations – because Noel was minus his TV. It was a major catastrophe when it broke down, but again we found how wonderfully kind people could be. I had hardly put the phone down from ringing our local TV man before he was on the doorstep. Noel invariably greeted him in a doleful voice with 'My telly broken, you will mend it.' When the job was done (having never taken his eyes off him throughout the whole operation) he said to me, 'Very good man, Mummy – telly OK now!' He was never without one – as if a major fault cropped up, which was very seldom, we were loaned another set immediately. Noel was happy to have his own set back though.

All quizzes and games he loved watching, especially *Sale of the Century* and *Opportunity Knocks*. *This is Your Life* was another highlight of his week, and if he knew the person involved this was a real bonus. He would be saying all through 'Give him (or her) the book!' I wish I had a pound for every time my husband and I said with real feeling, 'Thank God for the television set.' It was a life-saver for Noel.

It was a very long time before he took to radio. He wouldn't listen and just kept saying it was 'queer', 'Where is the man?' etc. Yet when in hospital he would let the nurses put his earphones on and he'd listen to the music. Amazingly enough, when his 21st Birthday came along he wanted a watch and a wireless of his own,'(he never called it a radio). So we complied, and he loved it because it was his. He was able to switch it on and off himself and he put it on every morning – yet keeping one eye on the clock for when it was time for the television to go on. No doubt which was his first love!

Noel would lend Daddy his 'little wireless' to take to work

when the cricket was on, but was very firm about 'You must bring it back!'

We did all we could to keep Noel happy and stimulated and at least he never lacked love or company, even if he did have more than his share of suffering. If his life in the latter years settled into a 'sameness pattern' it was because we'd run out of ideas!

10

Work

However can this word and what it stands for apply to Noel? Well, when he had all his 'bits and pieces' he was quite a busy little person, always scuttling around and prying into odd corners and quite often coming up with something with which to amuse himself or do. He especially loved to think he was helping me. I never had to fold the washing – he did it to perfection, with all the handkerchiefs, tea-towels, pillow cases and dusters etc in their own pile. Some of his help, or 'work', as he called it, did misfire at times, especially in the garden (when he was doing work for Daddy!) – but not for lack of effort. It was certainly a 'clean sweep'. The broad beans and 'funny beans' were often prematurely picked during his early years.

The day he decided to clean the bath was rather disastrous, from the amount of Vim used to the flooding of the bathroom floor. When his mind was set on a bit of polishing, the polish was spread on thickly, but of course not sufficiently rubbed in – so we either skidded or stuck! During the years we kept chickens he loved to see them being fed and insisted on helping – especially if 'Old Dad' was feeding them.

Each school holiday that came around I tried to catch up on spring? cleaning – my spring usually extended through the year! – and then Noel was in his element. When he was mobile he'd sort out and stack things up and be a real help – always telling me to do more work! Even when he was confined to bed he'd insist, every holiday, that I sorted out the pantry which led off his room. This always cheered him immensely. He'd watch me with the eye of a hawk and wouldn't let me throw anything out unless he'd had a look at it. (He was always very concerned, as his toys and posses-

sions not in current use were stored under the stairs in the pantry.) He demanded all the books, puzzles, games etc. to be put on the bottom of his bed – and he'd check and pack them up again into the boxes, all with one arm and his 'little one'. When Daddy came home he was regaled with how much work we had done. When I'd had an extra-busy day, I was usually rewarded by Noel saying, 'You are good Mummy – lots of work today.'

My baking days gave him great pleasure and invariably brought forth the remark 'Lovely smell in my house, what you made today?' He enjoyed 'helping' when he was younger, even if he wouldn't try the end product.

Drawer tidying was another thing Noel loved doing. I used to empty it all out on the bottom of his bed and with a combined effort I think we did a good job – though Daddy often complained afterwards he didn't know where anything was! While Top Cat still retained her other name of 'Bossy Billy' over the years, Noel quite often was called 'Bossy Boots' – and rightly so. From his bed, even when not able to do anything himself, he constantly told us to 'get on with the work'. How I miss his bossiness – and his telling me to 'do the lot' when I was ironing. (I still can't leave anything in the basket.)

There's no doubt at all that even when Noel wasn't able to do much himself he enjoyed seeing others working. When he was able to have his French doors open he watched Daddy digging, cutting the lawns, planting etc. and became quite put out if his father popped in to see some sport on TV. He was invariably told, 'You must do the garden!' Poor Daddy – there was always so much that needed doing and of course 'Bossy Boots' to crack the whip!

At Christmas time he loved to help when I was doing the cards. He was able to write his own name after ours and helped in putting a few into envelopes. Try as I would I was never successful in persuading him to lick the stamps and put them on. Sellotape too was sheer anathema to him – 'Very terrible and sticky.' Each parcel I packed up was the prelude to the same question – who's it from? I never succeeded in getting the message over to him it was going 'to' someone. (I'd often encountered this problem in younger normal children.)

The regular callers to our house were usually asked by Noel what work they'd been doing, and in the days when groceries were delivered our grocer was told to 'take more boxes to lots of Aunties'. The newspaperman was asked to 'put the papers in the hole' – followed by 'and you do it again tomorrow!'.

There were days when Noel was bored, and the childish, 'What can I play with?' or 'What can I do?' rather sadly changed to, 'I want to work' in his latter years. I remember his last gesture of rebellion. He had had a bleed into his 'little leg' – not a bad one – and it was well on the way to recovery, but he still needed bed-rest. My husband and a friend were decorating the front of the house and Noel had seen the ladders being carried round. Thinking he was quite safe in his bed in his room downstairs and with the TV to interest him, I was doing a job in another part of the house. Imagine my surprise and horror when I saw Noel going along the hall on his bottom, little leg held aloft, just in his pyjamas, towards the front door. I halted his progress and asked him where he was going. The answer came, 'Me going up the ladder to help my Daddy.' It needed all the tact and persuasion my husband and I could summon up to get him back to his bed, and the next few days we waited with bated breath for another bleed to start. Amazingly enough it didn't.

Noel didn't like it if Daddy or I 'nodded off' in the evenings. He thought we should be doing something most of the time, even if it was only knitting, reading or talking. (Quite often we were too worn out to comply!) He was always so interested in what I was knitting and when I breathed a sigh of relief after sewing up a garment, Noel's comment was usually, 'All finished now, Mummy, very super!' He certainly wasn't stinting in his praise.

Noel was very fond of a friend of ours who helped us out with interior decorating. Uncle Mark became a real buddy and if Noel had had his way he would have become a permanent resident in our home. He played along when Noel was bossing him and called him 'The Boss'.

Although for many years Noel wasn't able to 'work' as he wanted to, he derived vicarious pleasure from watching others. I think if he had just been a mongol, without the haemophilia, he could easily have learnt a simple routine job. He certainly had the desire to work. But then, we humans are rather perverse beings, so perhaps if Noel had been fit he wouldn't have had such strong desires to work. Who knows?

11

Sport

Noel's love of sport was inherited from both my husband and myself. All through our life-time we've been sport mad. At school my reports always ended with the comment – 'If she put as much energy into her academic work as her sports, would do excellently!' My husband's were in the same vein. We felt so sad that Noel wasn't able to participate and use his natural tendencies. Melanie never showed much interest. Following us at the same school, she was expected to be like us, and being a bit of a rebel she turned anti-sport. After she'd left school she took up sports we'd never played!

From quite an early age we realised Noel had a good eye with a ball – and was able to catch and throw with accuracy. Naturally we were ever on the look-out to see he didn't do anything likely to cause bleeds – but it was virtually impossible. He wanted to do what a normal boy would do: kick balls, play darts (this was definitely out till we got some with rubber suction ends), have a game of cricket with Daddy, use one of my tennis racquets, and probably most frightening of all, wanted to shoot with Daddy's gun! We had an old table-skittles set and he was pretty good at that – but yet again the swinging ball could have caused extensive damage to him.

We were delighted when we found Noel enjoyed watching sport on TV. (Three cheers again for telly.) This helped a lot during his bedridden years. When there was a football match on, he chose the team he wanted to win, then we had the other one to make it more fun. He got very excited when 'the ball went in the hole' for his team and would clap his little arm and shout 'Good shot.' In contrast he became rather irate, with a few swear words thrown in, when they missed!

He was well aware how the games varied with the seasons of the year – accepting that he saw Rugby in the winter at the same time as 'kick-ball' – but he called it 'Funny kick-ball'. He thought it great fun to see the players covered in mud. 'Very mucky' was his description of them.

Summer he knew brought cricket and 'Mummy's tennis' (Wimbledon). He accepted that every available minute I would have that on. He was always much more amenable to my seeing tennis non-stop than Daddy turning over to another station for cricket. He was tickled pink when Nastase and various other players had the odd altercation with the umpire. He would shake his head and say, 'Terrible temper, Mummy.'

Whatever sport he was watching he always ended up by saying, 'Me do that one day.' The desire to compete was ever with him. During a cricket match he was constantly urging the batsman to 'hit a big one', and to run very fast. I'm sure in his mind he was running with them. When the table tennis championships took place he was delighted, never omitting to say, 'Me played that at my school.'

Noel's daddy had always been clever at juggling with balls, oranges etc. This really got Noel going, and after each performance he'd say, 'My Daddy do that on telly one day!' In his eyes Daddy could do everything – including being 'a very strong man'. (This followed weight-lifting competitions.)

Athletics provided Noel with much enjoyment, especially the pole vault, 'Right up to the sky', putting the shot, 'Man very giddy', and the long and high jumps. In the running we had to tell him who we wanted to win and their names. Invariably after watching running he commented, 'Me can't run with one foot.' Then came the oft repeated explanation – that it was 'a naughty foot' and had caused him lots of pain, so Mr Jones had taken the pain away. With lots of cuddles and diplomacy we usually averted tears and channelled his thoughts into another direction.

I don't suppose wrestling would really be classed as sport – but it certainly provided Noel with entertainment and again the competitive element between the 'good man' and the 'bad one' crept in. He loved the fat ones with a big belly, like Big Daddy and

Haystack and he would chortle with delight and wriggle and squirm as they performed their antics. Tag wrestling was almost too much excitement for him – especially when they were all in the ring at once.

Hockey he thought was 'all right' but the only part he really liked was when a goal was scored. Ice-hockey was too fast for him to enjoy watching. Netball and basketball were 'super' – 'Me like that!' The darts championships were greeted with great pleasure. Having played with 'safety darts' when young, he had a good idea of what was going on. He knew when the dart hit the middle of the board it was called 'the bull' and that it was a 'good shot' when it landed round the outer edge or in the trebles. If a dart ricocheted off a wire he would commiserate by saying, 'Bad luck, Uncle!'

Snooker was a real firm favourite – we've stayed up till the early hours many a time to see the end of a match. He was well aware that all the balls had to finish in the pockets and that the red ones had to 'go in the hole' first. When all the balls were sunk, he knew the man at the table was the winner and he received a 'Well done, Uncle.'

Cycle and car races had him almost ecstatic – especially when the cars were swerving round corners with screeching brakes. His torso gyrated each time in rhythm with them! He became rather upset when accidents occurred, yet accepted quite readily pile-ups in the jalopy and old banger races, especially when doors flew off and various other bits and pieces were scattered around. That was regarded as 'very funny' but the man had to be 'all right'.

Horse racing and show jumping were other delights to him, particularly the latter, when he constantly urged the horses to jump higher and higher and not fall down. He much preferred the 'Aunties' to win and was unstinting in his praise with 'Well done Aunty, you very good. You the winner!' During Noel's younger years when he was mobile we used to take him and Mel to our local point-to-point races – and they both thoroughly enjoyed them. There were usually tears or tantrums when it was time to go home.

The first sport that we ever saw on colour TV was golf, and this always remained one of his firm favourites; with all the disadvantages fate had dealt Noel, he was blessed with wonderful eyesight (more so than Melanie, who turned out to have short sight). He loved watching the flight of the golf ball and cheered loudly if it landed on the green – becoming even noisier when it trembled on the brink and went in, or not, on the final putt!

Quite often there was a commentary on the golfers' clothes, particularly their hats – these fascinated him. He never really worked out why they had so many 'funny sticks' – yet when they were stuck in a bunker he'd shout out, 'Use the other stick.' (He must have had some inkling!)

Ice-skating was described as 'very lubbly' – especially the pair skating. He was particularly thrilled when they skated with speed and did their spins. His usual comment was, 'My Melanie can do that.' That was the only sport he didn't think Daddy would be able to do! When the 'Aunty', 'Uncle' or 'Girl' had a slip on the ice, each received a loud, 'Bad luck' from Noel, followed by, 'You OK now', when he or she continued their performance.

Noel spent many happy hours during his life watching sport – and Saturdays were looked forward to especially in this respect. Though let's face it, whatever the day or time, if there was sport on any channel, in our house we'd be viewing it! I know one thing for sure, watching sport now isn't anywhere near as colourful and entertaining as when Noel was alive. His funny little comments are sadly missed.

12

Religion

Amazingly enough religion over the years meant quite a lot to Noel, not that we were ever an over-religious family, but he adored the hymn singing. When well, he'd toddle off happily with Mel each Sunday to our little local church to Sunday school. Mel was quite proud the first time she took him on her own, and said he behaved quite well, but would insist on joining in with the teacher when it was prayers – not with the correct words! When the church had to be closed from lack of support, they joined the chapel Sunday school. This suited Noel even more, as it was less formal and the hymns and choruses had so much more rhythm and zip. These he attacked with much vigour if not expertise. Before he was able to remember the words he would join in with just the last word of each line.
One of his favourites was:

> Rout them out, get them gone,
> All the little rabbits in the field of corn,
> Envy, jealousy, malice, pride,
> All if allowed in my heart would abide!

Obviously he hadn't a clue what this meant or was all about – but the tune must have appealed to him.
    Another chorus that had survived from my childhood which he also liked was the following:

> We're travelling to the Mansion on the Happy Day Express,
> The letters on the engine are J!E!S!U!S.
> The guard shouts 'All for Heaven'

> And we gladly answer 'YES'.
> So we're travelling to the Mansion,
> On the Happy Day Express.

He liked shouting the 'YES' best of all!

When people stood up to pray, other members of the congregation often joined in with a fervent 'God be praised' or 'Yes, Brother'. Noel was known to have said, 'Well done, Uncle, open your eyes,' or to emit a loud 'AMEN'.

He adored Harvest Festival services, seeing all the flowers and of course the food! The chapel congregations always seem to give their all in singing and this of course gave Noel bags of scope for his performance! (Poor Mel so often showed embarrassment.) We usually took soft sweets with us to keep him quiet when absolutely necessary.

Although the children went to chapel Sunday school we still remained basically a C of E family and received rather spasmodic visits from the then vicar of our parish – who admitted he didn't enjoy visiting 'sick people'! He arrived on one occasion when both the children were ill with bad throats. Mel, who was in her first year at school and seemed to pick up everything, was the more ill of the two. The vicar said to her, 'Poor Melanie, I expect you're bored,' and she mis-hearing or mis-interpreting, said, 'No, I'm not, my daddy's bald!' Noel would never have anything to do with him at all and when he was older described him as 'a big black bird'. Obviously not one of his darlings. His best-loved vicar was yet to come.

In hospital, Noel loved the people who came round with texts, tracts etc. and kept the pictures safely on his locker to eventually bring home with him. Anything vaguely connected with religion he just called 'God'.

When confined to bed, TV was always turned on at exactly the same time on a Sunday to get the first church service, this often being Communion. He was very intrigued by 'What was in the funny cup?' and when told 'sherry', he'd reply 'Me like that!' He did too. The wafers he decided were 'very little biscuits', He watched every detail of this service avidly and knew the exact sequence of events – as we found out many years later!

This came to light rather oddly during a power cut – in midwinter. Our heating system, depending on electricity to fire it, meant we had no warmth, or any way of having a hot drink. Noel especially was browned off with no telly, so he, Daddy and I were just wrapped in layers of clothes with virtually nothing to do except be patient. We did have candles and a lantern! Then Noel decided he was thirsty so we all had an orange drink. As time went on and still no electricity, I admit I too was getting really fed-up and almost on the point of dropping off to sleep – when I noticed Noel going through the same actions over and over again. I watched more carefully and at last it dawned on me what he was doing!

He had finished his drink and was holding the beaker in the crook of his little arm and wiping the rim of it with his serviette; next pretending to drink again followed by further wiping of rim of beaker, then he put it down by Charlie Cooper and made the sign of the cross! (This was repeated with Big Bird and Kermit Frog.)

The biscuit he'd been given, he'd broken into little pieces and each bit he ate was followed by more crossing of himself! I nudged my husband and we sat there watching him till he sensed we were looking at him and he giggled. When I asked, 'What are you doing Noel?' He replied 'Me God, on Sunday!' It was certainly done with all due reverence! We laughed so much, we forgot about the cold. (Noel was best off anyhow because he was in bed.)

I'd better relate the whole truth – Daddy and I were having a cuddle on the settee, while Noel was performing with his beaker, so whenever power cuts, candles etc. were mentioned, Noel always joined in with 'Oh yes, me remember me God, and Daddy and Mummy cuddling!' (This was usually accompanied by a wicked look.)

Apparently when he was at school he loved the Scripture stories and pictures and one Christmas was in a Nativity play (a very minor role) – but he thoroughly enjoyed it. The Christmas carols he adored, especially when they were played by Stone Village Band, brass section and all! They came into our home for many years and performed two or three carols for him. When Noel was asked what he wanted – it never varied – first, 'While shepherds watched their flocks' and after 'Nöel, Nöel'. The latter he regarded as his own special carol. ('That's me!')

The Advent calendar that Aunty Dor-dor gave him yearly was done regularly each morning,and he knew that as a 'door' was opened it meant another day nearer to Christmas. (For me it signified how many shopping days left!) Noel understood Christmas Day was a special day because it was the birthday of Jesus. He particularly loved the pictures of Jesus as a baby.

Though he didn't understand what Palm Sunday was all about, he knew it was a happy day with all the singing and waving of branches – but thought Jesus looked very funny on a donkey! Noel regarded as one of his special treasures the palm cross he'd been given when he attended church Sunday school. It really was amazing how it survived over the years, and never got thrown out.

Easter Sunday was looked forward to eagerly, obviously with Easter eggs in mind, but he used to say, 'Very sad on telly, Mummy, Jesus dead, no come back no more.' He never enjoyed the Easter weekend TV overmuch. He always associated God with the sign of a cross, and wherever he saw one, on a bible, prayer book, in a picture or if he made one with his Lego or mosaics, his stock comment was, 'That's God.'

Funnily enough, the last six months of his life he kept on about 'wanting a God'. At last the penny dropped. He'd always admired the cross Melanie wore. It was Mel who asked him, 'Do you want one like mine?' The answer came in the affirmative, so she bought him one for his birthday – his twenty-eighth only 17 days before he died. He was very happy to have his 'God' and wore it continuously, but was rather distressed one morning when he woke up to find, as he thought, it had gone; but the cross had slipped round the chain to the back of his neck. He was so pleased to have his 'God' back. Melanie has it now.

I still have a vivid picture in my mind of Noel conducting the hundred favourite hymns on a Sunday with his 'little arm' and becoming even more jubilant when it was anything performed by the Salvation Army. He was very complimentary to them.

Such simple pleasures, but meaning so very much to him. Noel's innocence was the very essence of 'goodness'. There was no deception in him at all. It always made us so sad that whenever he was in bad pain he'd say, 'I've been so good, Mummy', as if thinking he was being punished for something. He certainly had a very big cross to bear during his life-time, and if there is such a thing as reincarnation (my husband believes strongly there is), I only hope he'll get a better deal next time.

13

Holidays and 'Special days'

All Noel's holidays took place up to about the age of 14. After that it was becoming more and more difficult to lift him around. Apart from the fear of starting bleeds, he had become quite a weight.

During the very early years of his life we spent most of our holidays with relations or friends. Amazingly enough we often had some very happy times with nothing really untoward happening, but naturally there were the odd bleeds.

Fortunately he was a good traveller, being quite content to look at everything around him, whether sitting in the back of the car with Melanie, or in any other form of transport. One holiday we spent near Hastings, and as we had no car then we'd travelled by train to London; then had to cross town by taxi to get our connection for the last stage of the journey. We arrived early evening after a rather exhausting day. Noel, who hadn't been walking very long, started off the holiday by falling down a flight of stairs (well carpeted, thank goodness!) and sustained no injuries at all! He just rolled over and over like a ball. We couldn't believe our luck. Lady luck stayed on our side all that holiday and the journey home passed without mishaps too.

Our caravan holidays varied from good to bad, with many shades between. We found Noel settled in quite well into this environment, except that he was wont to wander off into other people's abodes if we took our eyes off him for a minute. Some times we were lucky with the caravan being situated near the beach, but mostly not – so this meant Daddy usually had to give him a piggy-back down to the sand. This wasn't too bad but the 'up' journey was the problem. The paths were never wide enough to accommodate his wheelchair.

One of the places we stayed at in Devon was an old 'gun-site' position and the path to the beach had to be seen to be believed. On arrival we found our caravan was called It'll Do. No truer words existed. All one can say was – it was a shelter! Melanie, then about eight, went around looking at what was there, exclaiming, 'What's this?' and unfortunately knocked the fold-up table on Noel and started a bleed. That holiday was a disaster from start to finish, culminating with both children going home 'lousy' – just for full measure. Don't ever hire a caravan called It'll Do – it won't!

Whatever the sea was like, calm and like a millpond or rough, or however hot the day, we could never tempt Noel into it. He shrieked like a banshee even if his father held him up in his arms. We gave up trying after a time. He loved digging in the sand but hated it when it stuck on him. His domain was a groundsheet – and he made sand castles all the way round the perimeter and when that was completed started a second row – and so on as far as he could reach without leaving the safety of the cover.

Beachballs were super for him, as they were comparatively soft, although rather large. Mel, Daddy and I spent a lot of time chasing them for him. The little monkey looked in one direction then threw in another. Mel often took to the water for respite.

He loved watching the big boats out at sea, the antics of the other children in the water and people playing cricket on the sand, yet wouldn't move an inch on to the sand himself. Over-boisterous dogs upset and frightened him.

There were the occasions on holiday when Noel had visible bad bruising. I remember one incident very distinctly. He was considerably bruised on his back, and as it was an exceptionally hot day was only wearing a little pair of trunks. People looked at him, then at us in a mixture of disgust and horror and obviously thought we were child-beaters. Quite soon we had a patch of beach to ourselves. My husband and I were very upset and hurt, but tried to console each other by remembering that people who knew us were well aware of our true feelings towards Noel. We couldn't just go up to strangers and explain. From the age of four he wore a disc on his wrist telling the world he was a haemophiliac. This proved to be a great help. Thirty years ago his complaint wasn't so widely talked about as now and when it did crop up in conversation, at least 70 per cent said, 'Never heard of it.'

I think the years between five and nine were probably some of the happiest years in Noel's life. (Probably because he was mobile.) Of course there were bleeds and bad patches with periods of pain, but the proportion of good and bad patches came down slightly on the good side. We certainly had some good holidays during that period.

We weren't over-flush with money in those days, but by saving sixpences throughout the year in Haig dimple jars (a full one produced about £32!) we were able to get away most years, usually in a hired car. Our first 'old banger' let in the rain over the front passenger seat, so I was the one who got wet, but we were able to laugh about it. We didn't feel, however, it was roadworthy enough to take us to the seaside.

We had one super holiday, just over the border into Cornwall. A friend of ours had a cottage on the bank of a river. He owned a motorboat and from the word go, Mel was longing for a trip in it. She had been promised she should, though we were doubtful about Noel. He, however, had made up his mind he was going too, so we rather reluctantly gave in. He was in a fairly fit phase, but alas also a mischievous one! So clad in a life-jacket he joined the rest of us for a trip on the river. We were hardly under way before he started thumping his chest and saying, 'Me Billy Bunter.' Next he decided to have a go at our friend's beard and, not content with that, he threw his woolly cap in the water! So it continued till we were back on terra firma. I was never more thankful in my life. Why he didn't fall overboard, I shall never know. I must say we had some laughs that holiday – even if there were times when I suffered from palpitations!

Several happy holidays were spent with very good friends of ours who live near Marlborough. They live in a thatched cottage, near a farm. This really suited Noel, though he wasn't too enamoured by the 'creepy-crawlies' that came in from the thatch at night-time! The geese and gander that walked round during the day usually sent Noel scuttling away to us for protection. On wet days he spent most of his time playing (opinions varied on this) the piano – only being prised away for food!

It was during one of these holidays that Aunty Pat nearly choked. She got something stuck in her throat and could hardly breathe. We had to bend her over and thump her back for quite a time before she recovered. Noel was very frightened and whenever we mentioned Aunty Pat in later years, he always went into a mime of how she coughed and choked.

We had rather a funny incident on our journey home from the same holiday. We'd hardly left Aunty Pat's before Noel kept saying he wanted to do 'a potty'. We talked him out of it for a time but realised eventually it was becoming urgent and had to stop – unfortunately on a clearway. Noel was sitting on his potty on the back seat of our car when a police car pulled up. We groaned and thought, now we're for it. Fortunately for us the policeman saw the funny side of the situation, grinned and said, 'Tell him to get a move on and then move yourselves as quickly as possible.' We did, with Noel saying, 'Very lubbly 'liceman!'

When holidays became impossible we found days out the next best thing. Noel loved his visits to Bristol Zoo (where he wanted to spend all his time at the monkey temple). We pushed him around in his chair and he was in his element. He wasn't so fond of the big cats but adored the elephants and so badly wanted a ride on one. That was out, of course. The penguins he found fascinating and he loved seeing the animals fed, especially the seals.

We visited Bristol as regularly as we could as his Granma and Aunty lived there and then there were the trips to Weston, where another aunt and uncle lived. These were happy visits because we usually went down to the sea. After our first old banger we graduated to an Austin A40 pick-up. This we found very handy for piling Noel's chair and other bits and pieces in and it took us many times to Weymouth, where we always seemed to find sunshine. Not so Minehead; our visits there soon ceased. Nothing ever seemed to go right and the weather was generally inclement.

We spent many happy hours on the banks of the River Severn, and every sunny weekend that Noel was well and there was nothing else on, we had picnics there with a group of our friends. This was before Noel's foot operations, and Melanie and Daddy spent quite a bit of time fetching him back from his walk-abouts. He was always on the spot though, when it was time for food!

Noel got a tremendous kick out of weddings, and whenever any of our close associates and friends had any in the family they came in their regalia to see him. (This was when he was laid up.) Melanie's first wedding provided him with plenty of entertainment and he boosted her confidence no end by reiterating almost continuously, 'You very super, Melanie. Lubbly frock and flowers' – but he couldn't take to the veil. The celebrations suited him down to the ground.

Birthdays in the family, especially his own, he adored; treasuring all the cards for years. One birthday stands out very vividly in my mind – it was mine and Noel was seven coming up to eight. He looked at all my presents, among which was one from Melanie, and then burst into tears. We were dumbfounded and couldn't understand what was wrong, then amid sobs he stammered out, 'Me want to give my mummy a present.' Daddy always made sure every year afterwards that Noel had one to give me, though more often than not he told me what it was before I'd started to undo the first layer!

Noel was usually sad when his actual birthday was over and made the same comment each year, 'My birthday all gone now.' A rather odd thing happened on his very last one. I've mentioned somewhere previously that he always had a birthday cake simply in order to blow out the candles. Well, I was quite sure I'd checked I had the correct number of new candles to put on his cake – this being 28 – but when the time came I only had 27 and with no chance at all of getting to the shops for more. I looked around and found one that had been used the year before and was in good condition. I put this on where it would be least noticed, but of course I knew it was there and felt annoyed. One of my friends told me afterwards it was considered to be bad luck to use a candle that had already been blown out. Strange it was his last one.

New Year's Eves were very special to him; the telly was on even longer than usual, the hogmanay celebrations were lively and merry and he was allowed a small drink to welcome in the New Year. He normally managed to be the first to say 'Happy New Year' to all and sundry. He understood really well the passing of days, weeks and months. This knowledge had grown over the years, as on one of his birthdays he'd been given a roll calendar. It was Daddy's daily duty to perform the ritual of turning on the day, date and month and showing each one to Noel. He soon learnt the order of the days and, with more difficulty, the months, but he finally mastered them. The first day of each month was greeted with, 'Wabbits for luck!' Poor Daddy had such a telling-off if he inadvertently forgot to do it in the morning and was told to 'do it now' when he returned from work in the evening.

Mother's Day presented a bit of a problem. It was many years before he would accept it wasn't another birthday. I used to tease him and say I had to have lots of kisses and love all day, to which he replied, 'Me do love you, Mummy.' (The 'me' instead of 'I' persisted throughout his life-time.) Father's Day was even more of a mystery to him, and when I'd say, 'I'm going to do the washing-up' and Daddy didn't move, Noel got really cross and said, 'You must help my mummy.' (You can see whose side Noel was on!)

I suppose that every happy day he spent free from pain was a bonus and a special day for him, but obviously like all children (and Noel remained a Peter Pan till the day he died) his highlights of the year were Christmas and his birthday.

14

Clothes and Personal Belongings

From a very early age Noel was interested in his clothes and made valiant efforts at putting them on – but not always successfully, I hardly need add! He knew exactly which were his clothes and which were Melanie's and seldom made a mistake in that respect. He loved having new ones but was rather self-conscious when trying them on although always very appreciative, there being a shy little 'Thank you Mummy, very lubbly.' Whenever I had a spate of knitting and wanted to know what colour sweater he would like, he invariably asked for black – heaven knows why! (I certainly never complied with this.) We never understood why he said black because he knew all the colours from about the age of four – but throughout his life-time he insisted black was best. Even when crayoning or painting, black featured quite largely in his 'masterpieces'. Noel was once told he looked very smart – so for ever more when dressed up it was 'Me smart,' and if Mel were with him he said 'Mel very pretty.'

Woolly hats, scarfs and gloves weren't very acceptable to him, and he would secrete them in the most odd places in order not to wear them. Yet he had a real passion for ties, commenting he looked like his daddy. He liked being dressed in his best clothes when we were going visiting, especially if he and Melanie had similar jumpers or cardigans. I always enjoyed doing Fair Isle knitting, and when their sweaters were in the same basic colour, I always put a very distinctive motif on Noel's. I usually tried to avoid buttons and buttonholes if possible as he found them very difficult to cope with, especially when his arms were stiff, but he managed zips very well.

During his pre-school days he spent most of his time in dungarees, a safety factor when falling down, and the pockets were easily accessible to him. (Like all small boys', crammed with his treasures and often some of Mel's!)

He hated spilling anything on himself or falling down and getting plastered with mud and was so apologetic about it. Occasionally Noel had a bought sweater or cardigan, usually given him by some relative, and at one year at Christmas he had a hunting-red one. His immediate reaction when we put it on was 'Me Robin Redbreast.' Whenever he wore it we teased him and asked him to whistle and tweeter for us. (Robins visited him frequently at his French doors during the years he was confined to bed and were his favourite birds.)

When it came to underpants and vests he had a good collection of gay-coloured ones, while Daddy usually had blue or white. The reason for the big distinction being that Daddy, like all typical males, usually grabbed the first ones he saw in the airing cupboard! When older, Noel's face would be a study when spotting a pair of his on his father and would shout out, 'Mummy, my daddy's got my pants on! Take them off.' (I think he would have liked me to do just that at that precise moment.) Socks, too, were sometimes mislaid and turned up on Daddy.

Noel loved his first pair of proper long trousers, his comment being 'Me a man!' These had their especial advantage when he wore his artificial aid. From his early teens we had to have his trousers made as his spine was curving and he was becoming a rather awkward shape. We dressed him in his 'proper' clothes for as long as we could, even if he was only lying or sitting on top of his bed. Of course the latter years of his life he spent most of his time in his pyjamas and quite a bit of that period just wearing the jacket when he had bleeds into his legs. It was rather awkward getting the bottoms on in any case as over the last few years his little leg became permanently fixed straight and his good one was bent, with little knee movement.

His bed to him was virtually his kingdom – from which in the nicest way he bossed us all. Again he knew his own sheets and pillow cases – gay ones, naturally. His bedspread and curtains, for many years had birds on. (As mentioned previously, he loved all birds.) These had been purchased from the Society for the

Preservation of Birds. He was rather possessive of everything in his room. 'That's mine,' 'My clock, my calendar, my lamp, my telly,' etc. and even more so with Daddy, Melanie and me. Are you getting a feeling that Noel was spoilt? Too true, we did spoil him, but with what he had to put up with in the way of suffering and lack of mobility, he deserved every bit of it, and it all stemmed from the fact we loved him, and he returned our love.

His Aunty Ruth painted a picture for him and it was very special. The plants in his room were guarded jealously and it would be he who reminded me when they needed a drink! 'Leaves very funny, Mummy.' His plants never did exceptionally well, possibly because so much talcum was used around him, leaving the inevitable film on the leaves. However, flowers of all sorts he adored, wild and garden ones, so we tried to keep one of his vases near him filled with seasonal sprigs. Apart from the visual pleasure they gave him, he loved the different smells.

One of his twenty-first birthday presents was a table that could be adjusted to swing over his bed. Top Cat and Uncle Bernon had given him this, and extremely useful it was too. Noel was particularly fond of it as he could spread his cards out on it, or his jigsaw puzzles. One problem was that having completed a jigsaw I wasn't ever allowed to break it up and put it back in the box again, so the table grew in height with jigsaw upon jigsaw!

His own very personal things, such as towels, flannels, shaving soap, smellies, after-shave lotion, razor and shaving brush etc., were kept under strict vigilance by Noel. (Not very hard to guess who might have run out of his own!) On the odd occasion he did lend Daddy some of his 'smellies' he was instructed to 'bring it back after'. Noel always kept his own serviettes and the last Christmas he was alive he'd had two lovely ones given him with his name embroidered on. These he really treasured. One possession which never left his side was his purse! Any odd money he received was put in and the coins were counted religiously. He much preferred coins to paper money. He never really understood the different values, but enjoyed thinking he'd got lots of money and was quite a little miser in his way. He'd protest strongly if I wanted to take any out to buy him something special and say, 'There's some in your purse, Mummy.' He had the right idea anyway!

One thing about Noel, he really looked after his belongings and treasures and hated to discard anything. Even in his periodical clear-ups, very few items found their way into his waste-paper basket. There is no doubt at all that his puppets, who spent all the daytime hours on his bed, and at night slept in strict order (dictated by Noel) on the settee or floor of his room, were the most dearly loved, or at least on a par with his telly. We often commented if ever a burglar had broken into our house, he would have turned tail on seeing the line-up with Charlie Cooper, Big Bird etc. Favourite books that he'd had from a very early age were stacked on his shelf near his bed and gone through at intervals, mainly for the pictures, of course, but he was able to pick out a few words.

Never moving from its own very special spot was the sole relic from his schooldays: an iron or kettle holder that he had stitched and decorated himself. The pride in his voice when he said, 'Me made that and my darling Miss Spiers helped me,' I'm sure he set it above all else. Even Noel sensed the pleasure of personal achievement and a job well done.

15

...And Lovely Things

Noel very much appreciated lovely things and often found beauty in the most unexpected places. While he was confined to bed, his vista didn't cover a wide span, so we gave him as wide a one as possible by placing mirrors in strategic places. These enabled him to see us when we were in various parts of the ground floor, and the arrival of visitors – often before they saw him. New arrangements of flowers in the 'top hall' were always greeted enthusiastically as being 'very lubbly'.

Flowers gave Noel so much pleasure. From his earliest years when returning from a walk with Mel and her friends, he couldn't get in quick enough to present me with a bunch of wild flowers. He, ensconced in his pushchair, was laden with all their collections, but would never relinquish any of his bunch 'cos they were for his mummy. Mel and her gang were wonderful with him, often taking him along the scenic route to see the trains. They kept a pretty good watchful eye on him, though I've learnt of several incidents only recently when there had been a bit of trouble. Still, what the eye doesn't see, etc.

Living in the country was a godsend in so many ways. If the weather was reasonably clement, whatever the season, we took Noel out as much as possible, during his younger years. I'm so glad we did as he had many happy memories of his walks round Wick lanes. He was quite observant and we had to keep stopping because he'd spotted something. The first wild violets and primroses were smelt over and over again. I think he was very conscious of pleasing smells, almost as much as visual things.

He particularly loved the feel of the wind on his face, especially when Daddy was pushing him very fast, and in the autumn when the leaves were swirling he described them as 'very happy and dancing' and 'very pretty colours'. When the trees were being bent into strange shapes by strong winds, he was worried they'd fall down. Halls brook and Cockshot bridge provided Noel with much pleasure; these were yet two more stopping places for throwing stones in the water and watching the ripples and looking for small fish. Thousand upon thousand of leaves and paper boats must have wended their way down-stream too.

Noel always loved shapes, and trees with odd angled branches never ceased to fascinate him. He so badly wanted to climb trees before his amputations, but naturally he never did Our next door neighbours' children had a tree-house (it still exists) in a blasted elm. They got up to it via a Tarzan rope and Noel would watch their antics and at least got vicarious pleasure.

I think I mentioned earlier that he was an inquisitive sort of child and blessed with good eye-sight was often fascinated by some of the smaller species of life – things found under pebbles, in odd corners of the garden and in the grass and bushes etc. I remember his delight in showing me a ladybird he had cupped in his hands and when he saw his first grasshopper, he tried to copy its movements. He didn't like me killing anything, with the exception of wasps. Having been stung badly once, they were regarded as 'terrible wappies'.

Each season brought Noel pleasure in varying ways, especially during his laid-up years. The open sesame to the outside world was via his French doors and, believe me, these were opened virtually at first light and not closed till the last possible minute every day, going on right through into autumn, till we were forced to close them for the winter months ahead. He hated it when this happened and always said, 'You will open them again one day!'

Rain was termed 'terrible weather' by Noel and fog frightened him because he couldn't see anything, but snow and frost he found quite fascinating. The heavy hoar frosts he was quite enchanted with – 'Trees very lubbly, Mummy, Jack Frost did that' – and the very hard winters when his French doors were thickly coated he loved the swirling ice-patterns on the panes. He was always interested in the footprints in the snow of animals, birds and humans and was so happy when the robins and other birds visited his bird table, right near the French doors. The bird table was perhaps one of the focal points during the winter months. We had quite a wide range of birds who came to feed and the tits swinging on the lumps of fat and squabbling among themselves made him chuckle. He wasn't so partial towards starlings, thinking them 'naughty birds' and 'very greedy'. He loved watching the birds flying and going over in flocks and knew the difference when his cousin's pigeons flew over.

He was usually the one to hear the first call of the cuckoo, and this would be repeated by him almost non-stop for several days, but he never actually saw one. Nest-building time gave him lots of fun. Our garden provided plenty of scope for nests. He enjoyed seeing the birds with different bits and pieces in their beaks and thought they were 'working very hard'. We showed him some old empty nests and he was really intrigued with them and examined them from every angle. Noel was pleased to think he was helping when he told Daddy, 'Terrible birds eating the apples!' yet he didn't like it when his father shot at the wood pigeons who year after year ruined our green stuff.

The sky was a never-ending source of interest to him during the day-time and at night. He was fascinated by the clouds and seldom a day went by without some comment from him, especially when aeroplanes disappeared behind them and then reappeared. He thought the contrails made by the planes were 'lovely patterns' and 'very pretty'. For many years he expressed the wish to go up in a plane, but sadly that wish too never materialised. Helicopters he thought 'queer' and finally christened them 'funny planes'. He loved it when they came down low, and even enjoyed the noise! Sunset, especially when it had been a gorgeous day, with the sun going down like a ball of fire and the sky looking all rosy held him entranced. His French doors faced westward, so he had a wonderful view. Perhaps one of his most exciting moments came when he saw his first hot-air balloon. The colours were very vivid and luckily it took a long time to pass. The questions I had to answer about that!

He appreciated the night sky too – the stars and the moon – and called the full moon 'a fat moon'. He asked many times over the years who lived up in the sky, and on several occasions when he saw shooting stars, he wanted to know where they'd gone and told Daddy to 'go and find them'. The one particularly bright star – the evening star – he thought was shining specially for him 'There's my star.'

When he was young, Bonfire Night was a complete and utter delight to Noel. He loved the patterns the fireworks made in the sky, and the smoke and flames of the bonfire; even enjoying holding a sparkler at full arm's length. He never could understand though why the Guy being burned had one of Daddy's jackets on! During later years he watched the proceedings through his French doors. Lightning held no terrors for him, in fact he liked it, but he was afraid of thunder when it was particularly loud. Much as he hated rain, he nearly went mad with excitement each time he saw a rainbow – 'very lubbly colours' – and he'd name most of them. These probably seem such trivial pleasures to the normal person, but they meant so much to Noel and we were delighted he could relate to nature and beautiful things around him. Of course during his life-time he had far too much inactivity but he made the most of what was available and appreciated the important things in life. Although physically and mentally handicapped, I would rate his disposition as a hundred per cent plus.

We always knew when Noel was getting better after a bleed because the first thing he wanted to do was to look out of his French doors, and then if at all possible have them open – to see what was happening in the outside world and to draw in huge breaths of fresh air. He loved the smell of freshly cut grass and when all the lawns were cut was very complimentary to his father, 'You are good Daddy!'

The back of our house is covered with Virginia creeper and this grew round Noel's French doors in profusion. He was so pleased when the leaves came again in the spring and often encroached into his room. I told him once they'd come to see him, and he remembered this each year. He wasn't so pleased when they blew off in the autumn, though he loved the colours and movement. He had enough intelligence to know when all the leaves were gone it would soon be winter and that meant closed doors – but it also meant Christmas wasn't too far off!

Not all his lovely things were out of doors. When the Christmas tree was festooned and the decorations up, including lots of balloons, he would repeat almost non-stop, 'My room very lubbly.' We had quite a battle when the time came for taking everything down, though he was a little consoled by having all the Christmas cards. These he always put into two piles – one contained the ones he liked and the other was for the 'terrible ones!' – and so they remained.

Noel, like most of us, seemed to be revitalised when spring came round each year. He had his own special garden trough filled with spring bulbs outside his French doors and was very thrilled when he was able to say, 'Yellow daffodils and red tulips.' Uncle Bert taught him to say that.

Summer-time brought the butterflies, which were another source of interest to him. Having buddleia and ice-plants, we attracted quite a wide variety. Noel thought the butterflies were pretty when they 'sat on the flowers' and the odd one that flew in and settled on his bed brought squeals of delight. He knew the difference between butterflies and moths and, like his mother, was scared of the latter – particularly large ones. When his doors were shut and they beat against them in the evening he'd say, 'Me very happy, terrible moff outside!' (I knew how he felt!) Bats didn't come into his 'lovely' category either.

One evening 'something' flew down the chimney into Noel's room and settled in the corner behind the television. He and I were on our own and as we looked at each other he said, 'What's that, Mummy? Very terrible.' Viewing it from as far off range as I could, I realised it was a bat! Not wanting to upset Noel, I played it as cool as possible and hastily fetched Daddy from the garage to cope with the situation. Noel dived under his bed-clothes and I retreated rather cowardly to another room. Daddy carried out the operation of removal without much enjoyment either – but couldn't lose face!

Tall Aunty Maureen (of the exercise fame) after a holiday in Cornwall had brought Noel some shells and pebbles home and these he treasured and thought of as some of his 'special lovelies'. They were rather unusual ones. Alan, Aunty M's husband, did delightful carvings in wood and serpentine. Noel loved to touch and stroke these.

As he grew older he learnt to apply the word 'lovely' to people, pictures and more abstract things. He was very definite on his views on which people he thought were 'lubbly', He was always attracted by ones with blonde hair, and when the Miss World Competition was on he'd pick his blonde and stick by her. When I'd had a hair-do, he was always the first to comment and then ask for Daddy's approval too.

He loved looking through glossy magazines and choosing his 'very lubbly' pictures and cutting them out as long as he was able. (Many of his choices would have been mine too.) I was always so pleased he found joy in beautiful things and could discriminate between beauty and ugliness. Maybe he was imbued with the gift of seeing the world through rose-coloured spectacles in his good patches of health. Fate at least handed him out a lovely nature and the ability to derive pleasure from simple things. In some ways these must have helped to compensate for all the other set-backs.

16

The Final Tally

So, what's it all about? Was Noel's span of time on earth worthwhile? I have no hesitation whatsoever in answering that in the affirmative. His courage, his level of endurance and the love he gave us made him very special in our eyes, and there's no doubt he endeared himself to many, many other people as well, in all walks of life.

I must admit when I first realised something was wrong with him, and later when this was confirmed, I thought it was a cross we'd possibly find hard to cope with. In the beginning my sense of duty, which has always been strong, took over. After all, we were responsible for Noel's existence and he couldn't help being as he was. As it says in the Bible, 'What have ye, ye have not received?' We all start off life with a big question mark hanging over us, but I think Noel must have had a few exclamation marks as well! However, as the months and years went by, Noel's own personality emerged and he earned our love, which grew with time, and what he gave to us beggars description.

I know that in all honesty we couldn't have given more of ourselves physically and mentally to him, but looking back one always feels dissatisfied and has some regrets. The last few months of Noel's life I was in a poorish patch of health and felt very tired. I so often wonder if there were any 'pointers' along the way I missed. I was normally right on the ball. In retrospect I realise now he didn't want us out of his sight and in the evening when we were settled in to watch TV he kept telling Daddy to sit back 'cos he wanted to see his mummy. When I asked him what was wrong he'd shrug his shoulders and say, 'I don't know.' He was able to differentiate between the degrees of pain (little one, big, very big or terrible one) or ache, as applied to teeth etc., and 'I'm not very well' when he had a temperature or felt sick, but I don't think he could describe how he felt when he had 'odd' feelings as opposed to his normal pains. No doubt his heart, which had taken such a pounding over the years with his terrifically high pulse rates from bleeds (on one occasion in hospital it couldn't be charted as it was 'off the page' numberwise) had been affected more than we realised.

About two months before he died he cried out one night and when we went to him he said he was frightened, so we cuddled and reassured him and stayed with him till he went off to sleep again. I thought some creature outside might have made an odd noise and disturbed him, but when I asked him if a terrible cat had frightened him he said, 'No, very queer.' I have no doubt at all now in my mind that he'd had a 'fluttery' or irregular heart beat and felt, as he said, 'queer'. There were no repercussions after his 'being frightened' episode and we wrote it off as just one of those things.

Noel had been prone to patches of indigestion, which we thought were due to his inactivity and being laid down so much. He had medicine and tablets to alleviate it, but there had never been a suggestion it was anything to do with his heart. The attacks had occurred more frequently over the last year of his life, with the occasional bouts of sickness – but we assumed these were due to his liver condition and accordingly cut him down on fats.

I often torture myself by going over every little detail of the last few weeks of his life and particularly the last night. The weekend before he died he thoroughly enjoyed his Sunday dinner and said at bed-time, 'Very happy day, Mummy.' We got as much pleasure out of cuddling Noel as he did, but he seemed to want even more than normal and constantly said, 'You do love me very much' – in a questioning tone of voice. We couldn't have told him or shown him more how much he meant to us.

When I think of the number of times we'd been told there was no hope for Noel and we'd waited for the end, but he'd survived – yet when it did come it was so quick it caught us unawares. Of course we knew he was very ill. We'd asked our own doctor to come out (This was another Dr W who had entered his life over the last three or four years. He was very compassionate and gentle. Noel loved him too and oft admired his hair and choice of ties.) Noel had an injection to stop the vomiting. We never dreamt it was the last time we'd hear him say, 'I'm a poor old man.' We stayed up with him all that last night, 'cat napping' for the odd minute or so when he was quiet, but always there, to give him sips of water, sponge his sweats, cuddle him and I hope give him comfort. Any more details I just can't go into; suffice to say the last word he ever said was 'Mummy' as I held his head, and it didn't penetrate then that he was slipping from us. The next time I looked at him, he was gone. What a mixture of feelings swept over us. Initially, shock and disbelief of what we saw, then came gratitude that he was no longer suffering and relief that we had out-lived him and not he us. Overwhelming all was an immense sadness and a feeling of tremendous loss. Noel had been the nucleus of our lives for 28 years. Would we ever be able to form another pattern for living? Our Peter Pan had left us.

The very first person to come to see us when the news of his death got around was 'the man with the collar' and as usual we derived great comfort from him. Although he was then retired from his duties, we felt we wanted him to take part in Noel's funeral service. (Noel had loved him so much.) So, a word in the ear of the new vicar and all was arranged. We were very humbled by the number of people who came to the service and who wrote to us. Noel's last day on earth was flooded with sunshine and there were flowers in profusion.

Both his Dr Ws came to his funeral. Charlie Cooper had a Viking one.

It is now three years since we lost him, but there is seldom a day when something doesn't crop up that brings him vividly to our minds. His voice seems to linger as much or more than his presence.

It really took us a very long time to get used to a different life style, and many, many months elapsed before we started to sleep more deeply. I suppose the habits of virtually a life-time can't be erased in one fell stroke. Even now, any sound during the night and my mind immediately registers 'Noel' – but then reality takes over and I must admit relief floods in. We really were stretched almost to the limit of our endurance during the last couple of years of his life. As a very close friend of mine said to me afterwards, 'Seems as if someone, somewhere, was taking care of all of you.' Without question Noel had far more than his share of suffering – but some compensation was the love he received. As time has gone by we find we tend to remember the pleasant episodes of his life – few though they were – and the unpleasant ones are beginning to recede. He was truly a well-beloved son and still is.

I think I would have to say that on the whole it has been good therapy for me, writing this memoir to Noel.

Now, we're in another phase of our lives and I feel quite strongly we must make the most of our remaining years. We are gradually settling into a more relaxed way of living, having time to chat to passers-by, to stand and stare and to go shopping together on Saturday mornings. Love of the simple, small things has rubbed off Noel on to us.

Perhaps Noel and his almost life-size puppets supplied the ground work for my post-retirement years, as I'm now a fully fledged member of our local drama society. So many times when I've been making up my face, donning my wig and gear I've wished Noel could have seen me. (He'd have laughed uproariously!) Even more so, when treading the boards as one of the Ugly Sisters in pantomime. How wonderful it would have been, on looking down at a full house, to see his puckish face looking up at me and later hear the oft repeated words 'You very super, Mummy.' I hope I was, Noel.